CHANTICLEER

WITHDRAWN

Bell's Woodland

BELL'S RUN CREEK

WATERWHEEL

POTTING SHED

Orchard

Cut Flower and Vegetable Gardens

er Woods

Tennis Court Garden

Long Border

Parking Lot Garden

CHANTICLEER HOUSE AND TERRACES

ENTRANCE

LE SE

Teacup Garden

THE ART OF GARDENING

The Art of Gardening

DESIGN INSPIRATION AND INNOVATIVE PLANTING
TECHNIQUES FROM CHANTICLEER

R. WILLIAM THOMAS

with Eric Hsu, Dan Benarcik, Peter Brindle, Bryan Christ,
Doug Croft, Fran DiMarco, Joe Henderson, Ed Hincken,
Erin McKeon, Lisa Roper, Emma Seniuk, Anne Sims,
Scott Steinfeldt, Przemyslaw Walczak, and Jonathan Wright

Photographs by Rob Cardillo

TIMBER PRESS
Portland, Oregon

Acknowledgments

We would like to thank all who have ever been a part of Chanticleer, especially Adolph and Janet Rosengarten, the Chanticleer Board, and the Chanticleer staff (full-time, part-time, seasonal, and volunteer); Christopher Woods for developing Chanticleer from a pretty estate to an amazing public garden; Eric Hsu for his correction of nomenclature, editorial comments, review of photos, and writing of captions; and Ann Brown and Gari Brindle for their diligent editing.

PAGE 1 Bowman's root (*Porteranthus trifoliatus*), a North American species, has loose panicles of ethereal white flowers. PAGES 2–3 The Gravel Garden rolls into late spring with the last hurrah of bulbs, including *Allium hollandicum* 'Purple Sensation'. PAGE 5 The scented blossoms of sweet pea (*Lathyrus odoratus* 'Matucana') are a delight for eye and nose.

All photos by Rob Cardillo except those on pages 13 and 14 (courtesy of the Chanticleer Foundation), 55 top right (Lisa Roper), 56 (Lisa Roper), 81 (Jonathan Wright), 92 (Lisa Roper), and 262 (Lisa Roper).

The Haseltine Building
133 S.W. Second Avenue, Suite 450
Portland, Oregon 97204-3527
timberpress.com

Printed in China

Text design by Laura Shaw Design, Inc.
Cover design by Anna Eshelman

Library of Congress Cataloging-in-Publication Data

Thomas, R. William (Roger William), author.
    The art of gardening: design inspiration and innovative planting techniques from Chanticleer/
R. William Thomas with Eric Hsu, Dan Benarcik, Peter Brindle, Bryan Christ, Doug Croft, Fran
DiMarco, Joe Henderson, Ed Hincken, Erin McKeon, Lisa Roper, Emma Seniuk, Anne Sims, Scott
Steinfeldt, Przemyslaw Walczak, Jonathan Wright; photographs by Rob Cardillo.—First edition.
        pages cm
    Includes index.
    ISBN 978-1-60469-544-1
    1. Gardens—Pennsylvania. 2. Gardens—Design. 3. Chanticleer Gardens (Wayne, Pa.) I.
Cardillo, Rob, photographer. II. Title. III. Title: Design inspiration and innovative planting
techniques from Chanticleer.
    SB466.U7C435 2015
    635—dc23
                                                                                    2015014313

A catalog record for this book is also available from the British Library.

Contents

An autumnal view toward the Pond Garden's Rock Ledge and the Winter Shrub Border: Chanticleer's encore arrives through colorful autumn foliage and grasses (a streak of *Muhlenbergia capillaris* glimmers in the fading light).

INTRODUCTION

For some, the words *art* and *gardening* never mesh.

To them, art is something found in a museum, a theater, or a concert hall. Art outdoors might be a sculpture park, where the plantings are merely a background. But for the Chanticleer staff, art is an everyday experience. Our gardeners are artists in every sense of the word, and they work in all media from plants to paint, wood, stone, metal, and clay. Their artistic vision sees beauty in the plants, stones, water, and pavement as visual elements. They create a garden experience where scent, sight, color, sound, and texture combine to make three-dimensional works of art that continually grow and change.

Visitors are treated as guests of the Rosengarten family, so adults and children feel welcome to enjoy the garden for pleasure and relaxation.

PREVIOUS PAGE Difficult-to-grow Japanese wood poppy (*Glaucidium palmatum*) is a cool-loving woodlander cosseted for its lilac flowers.

Their endeavors may be compared to a chamber orchestra performance, where a number of soloists come together to produce a single, unified piece. At Chanticleer, the conductor is the head gardener/executive director, whose role is to meld the exquisite work each gardener produces into one unified production: the garden. For the past twelve years, I have had the pleasure and privilege to be that conductor at Chanticleer.

This book aims to be a conversation between our staff and you. All of our staff have contributed in some way to the book, and many wrote individual sections explaining how they garden or design their areas. Their biographies are at the back of the book, if you'd like to learn more about them. Our garden exists to inspire and is filled with ideas to try at home. We hope this book leads you to garden more frequently and freely. Chanticleer is our research laboratory where we try new plants, designs, and techniques all in the public view. Our guests see our successes and our failures, although we try to rush the losers to the compost pile. Horticulturist Dan Benarcik calls what we do "gardening without a net." You might want to do the same in your own garden. Try. And try again. Continue what you like. Move on to something else if you are displeased. Plant enough so the loss of one plant is not tragic.

WHAT IS CHANTICLEER?

Some people don't understand the Chanticleer experience. It's true, we are not easily pigeonholed, perhaps because of our unique confluence of art and horticulture. We aren't a typical botanical garden or arboretum. We're not a park. And we're not really a museum. We were once a private estate, and we like to keep the feeling of a private garden, but everything we do has the purpose of inspiring our guests.

One editor of a lifestyle magazine tried to figure out "what we are." He asked me:

Do you rent the space out?

No.

Do you do weddings?

No.

Do you have functions?

Occasionally for horticultural groups.

So, what is this place? Why do you exist?

We are a garden; a place of beauty, pleasure, escape.

But, I mean, what do you do? Why would anyone come?

Indeed.

But on further thought, perhaps I could have said: If we were a restaurant, we'd be trying new taste combinations with lots of local fare. If we were music, we'd be a chamber orchestra, playing classical and contemporary works, with each musician a soloist yet part of the ensemble. If we were a painting, we'd be an impressionistic landscape with a bit of abstract expressionism thrown in. If we were dance, we'd combine ballet with contemporary dance. But we're none of those. We're a garden. I guess you could call us performance art.

We don't rent out the property, allowing us to put all efforts into the garden for our guests. Instead of spending valuable staff time on events and rentals where the garden is merely a stage for the functions, we focus on the garden itself. We are called a "gardener's garden" because we are run by gardeners, designed by gardeners, and exist for gardeners.

Our founder, Adolph Rosengarten Jr. (1905–1990), called Chanticleer a "pleasure garden," and his description serves as our motto. The two words can be interpreted in many ways, but ultimately, we want our guests to leave in a better mood than when they arrived. People of all ages enjoy the property. Adolph Jr. commissioned a master plan that included one main path throughout the garden. Today, the path helps guests find their way, but we encourage them to leave the path, walk on the grass, and fully explore the garden.

There is no need to segregate kids into a children's garden here. We invite children to run from bench to bench, trying each one, to search for fish, frogs, turtles, and snakes by the ponds, and to roll down the Great Lawn near the main house. Teenagers appreciate the romance, the privacy, the just plain over-the-top quirkiness of the place. Spouses dragged here by the family's garden-lover find we aren't stuffy and it's actually not a bad place for a walk. Do-it-yourselfers enjoy the staff-made benches, chairs, gates, bridges, handrails, drinking fountains, and even our plant list boxes, which hold plant-identification handouts (in place of garden labels). Others find it is a good place for a date, to read a book, and even to find solace.

Chanticleer has been called the most romantic, imaginative, and exciting public garden in America. It is a contemporary garden within a historic setting. It is filled with colorful foliage and flowers—a learning garden demonstrating almost any type of gardening one might do in the region. We want our guests to feel welcome and relaxed, to find pleasure in the visit, and to return.

CHANTICLEER, THE ESTATE

Adolph G. Rosengarten Sr. was the grandson of a German immigrant who started a pharmaceutical business that eventually became part of Merck & Co. in 1927. In 1912, Adolph Sr. and his wife Christine purchased 7 acres in the western suburbs of Philadelphia that featured magnificent American chestnuts and a commanding view. The Rosengartens hired architect Charles Borie, a University of Pennsylvania classmate of Adolph Sr., to design their country retreat. The house was finished in August 1913 and the family moved in, returning to their Philadelphia home each winter. In 1924, they added rooms and converted the house into their year-round residence.

Landscape architect Thomas Sears laid out the terraces that remain essentially the same today, although with drastically different plantings. Soon after purchasing the property, the family lost most of the chestnut trees to chestnut blight, and planted the oaks, pines, and beeches we enjoy today. Chanticleer's oldest trees may be the black walnuts lining the walkway leading to the Potting Shed. They were large when the family moved here and Adolph Jr. believed they dated to the 1880s.

The Rosengartens named their home after Chanticlere in Thackeray's 1855 novel *The Newcomes*. Adolph Sr. enjoyed Thackeray and sympathized with the owner of the fictional Chanticlere, "mortgaged to the very castle windows [but] still the show of the county." *Chanticleer* is also a French word for rooster. Playing on the name, the Rosengartens incorporated rooster motifs throughout the property.

Adolph Rosengarten Jr. was a hands-on gardener who enjoyed pruning, including clipping hedges.

O. P. Jackson Jr. stands by a young oak (*Quercus ×saulii*) outside his mother Emily's house during the winter of 1962.

Adolph Rosengarten Jr. credited his interest in gardening to his mother and to his growing up at Chanticleer. His mother encouraged her children to plant a World War I victory garden at the site of the present-day swimming pool. Chanticleer's rolling hills, winding streams, and tall trees developed his artistic eye and inspired in him a desire to be a landscape architect. His father had a different idea, however, and told him the family needed a lawyer, so to law school Adolph Jr. went.

In 1933, Adolph married Janet Newlin, a serious gardener in her own right. They moved into neighboring Minder House (*minder* meaning less or small in German) and began creating their own garden. He wrote, "Lately my great interest has been in horticulture and landscape design." This interest was probably strengthened by his serving in World War II, stationed in England at Bletchley Park. Bletchley was a large estate with great lawns and stately trees, and no doubt strengthened his love of Chanticleer's rolling lawns and splendid trees.

Adolph Sr. and Christine gave each of their two children houses on adjacent properties as wedding gifts. Adolph Jr. and his wife's house, Minder, which they lived in until their deaths, was taken down in

1999 to build the Ruin. The senior Rosengartens built the house at today's Entrance to the garden for daughter Emily and her husband, Samuel Goodman, in 1935. After Mr. Goodman died, Emily married Orton Jackson Sr. Emily's House is now used as our administration and education building. Her three children and a granddaughter serve on the board.

Adolph Jr. took over ownership of the Chanticleer House and surrounding land following his mother's death in 1969 (his father had passed away in 1946). He used the house for entertaining but never moved into it, and kept it as it was when the family lived there. The house is in the center of Chanticleer, the public garden, and is our spiritual beginning. Adolph Jr. specified in the Chanticleer charter that the house is to be kept as a museum. We now open the house regularly for tours. During the 1970s, some of the surrounding estates were subdivided and sold. Janet and Adolph Jr. were strong proponents of preserving the property. Adolph Jr. wrote: "It seems a shame to break up what is now the most pastoral residential area in America into condos and future shopping malls. This beautiful countryside should be treasured." He continued, "One of the great joys of my life has been gardening. It's a wonderful way to express yourself. To create a garden is to search for a better world. Every gardener is like Oscar Hammerstein's Optimist, for the very act of planting is based on hope for a glorious future."

Adolph Jr. and Janet continued to develop Chanticleer and plan for its future. They oversaw the planting and maintenance of the trees and enjoyed a huge vegetable garden. Even though they had grounds staff, both enjoyed gardening. Janet was responsible for the flowers; her husband, the trees and shrubs. He received an award from the American Horticultural Society as "one of the foremost gardeners in the country." Adolph Jr. believed "a good garden is never static." Realizing he could not control the garden from the grave, he created a foundation in 1976 for the property and trusted the board and staff to guide its development. Chanticleer's executive directors have embraced the garden's history, but have not been limited by it. The garden is allowed to evolve and to be continually reinterpreted.

Our mission was spelled out by Adolph Jr. in the Chanticleer Foundation charter:

Operate the property as a beautiful public garden,
Maintain the Chanticleer House as a museum, and
Educate amateur and professional gardeners.

Chanticleer History in Adolph Jr.'s Own Words

In 1913, the only useable structure on the property was a small pre-Revolutionary dwelling to which father added a bathroom, now 810 Church Road. It was assigned to the chauffeur and his family. Nearby, a stable was built, with two stalls, spaces for three carriages and two automobiles, a hayloft, and a manure pit. A studio apartment was tacked on the back for a gardener or a groom, who would board with the chauffeur. This complex is now 812 Church Road.

The appearance of the property made it obvious that even rudimentary maintenance had not been a concern of the previous owners. The then fashionable landscape architect Thomas Sears was called in. His plan for "the big picture" centered on the magnificent American chestnut trees that had attracted my parents. Ten years later, the blight had killed these chestnuts. One feature of Sears's plan for the "little picture," the area nearest to the house, remains. On the south side, to match the roof, the architect put a wide slate terrace, from which the ground fell away. On the east the ground rose, ending in a knoll. This was dug into, and by extensive grading, a level area was made into a garden with beds, paths, and grass plots next to the house. Thanks to Sears, the formal garden at Chanticleer still appears to be an uncontrived extension of the house, while the house at times seems simply to belong to the garden. Without a house, a garden is merely a species of the genus museum; when taken together they form a holistic entity.

The work begun by my father and mother, who loved the place, was continued by my wife, whose indefatigable interest and impeccable taste not only furthered the enterprise, but also saved me from some horrid follies. My wife and I founded the Chanticleer Foundation for education of people from the city on how to landscape and keep places beautiful and attractive. People who move out from town don't know that if you put a Norway spruce in front of a window, it will grow up and you can't look out window.

Gardening is the most wonderful way of refreshing yourself. I have always loved horticulture, gardening, and improving. I am favored by providence with good health and a certain amount of wealth and I want to give back. Aesthetics in this part of the world have great attraction, an attractive rolling county with trees. I want to keep open space, to preserve this beautiful ground as much as possible.

A century ago, the property was a small farm, which must have been worked with difficulty for the ground undulates. Now the sheds and fields are gone, replaced during the last seventy years by lawns, flower and vegetable gardens, an embryonic meadow garden, a wild flower garden, a rock garden, and a stream-fed pond. On the north, two groves, one of native oak, ash, poplar, and walnut, the other of white pine and hemlock, serve as a screen.

A century later, when the Pennsylvania Horticultural Society, as its part in the Bicentennial, put on a series of symposia, we were honored when Chanticleer was chosen as a site for the fifth in the series. Many of the symposium participants joined the tours—despite the heat of a Saturday in mid-August—and many later wrote complimentary letters about the gardens. This brought home to us that sharing our enjoyment in the garden with others has its reward.

Thus, 1976 was the turning point [the year that Adolph Jr. wrote the charter for the Chanticleer Foundation], and thereafter our predilection for private life, gradually, but within limits, declined. We began to receive numerous requests to tour Chanticleer. We do no "marketing," believing that most people come voluntarily to learn about plants, landscape design, and good gardening practice, others to obtain the emotional satisfaction one gets from looking at a good painting, while the optimists hope for both.

Yoke-leaved amicia (*Amicia zygomeris*), a tender perennial from Mexico, has conspicuous maroon-veined stipules.

THE EVOLUTION OF CHANTICLEER GARDEN

The garden has changed greatly since 1990, when Adolph Jr. passed away and the Chanticleer Foundation (and therefore its board) took over management of the garden. When the garden opened to the public in 1993, we continued and expanded on Adolph Jr.'s basic plan. Under the visionary eye of the first executive director, Christopher Woods, the staff began developing garden rooms throughout the grounds. Chanticleer gained a reputation for gardening without rules and for expanding the boundaries of what "could" be done in the Philadelphia area. Magnificent trees and lawns remain as a living testament to the estate era, and newer plantings pay tribute to the love of gardening.

The change from a pleasant, green estate to a colorful, dynamic, and contemporary garden has taken years of evolution. Great trees continue to define, enclose, and frame the landscape. We plant more trees each year, regularly inspect all trees for pruning needs, and use extraordinary measures on the most significant trees including lightning protection. In today's world, damage to roots and to bark are the biggest causes of tree death. We avoid soil compaction, changes of grade, and root competition. Our groundskeepers carefully mow around trunks, using bladed trimmers less likely to injure bark than string trimmers.

Historic buildings and terraces likewise are important. We are conservative about changing an original physical structure. The Chanticleer Terraces, outside of Chanticleer House, remain much as they were when the Rosengartens lived here, except for the addition of a reflecting pool to the east and a new balustrade, matching the existing balustrades, at the overlook. At Emily's House near the Entrance, terraces retain their walls and an enclosed feeling, but a lean-to greenhouse is gone. The Teacup Garden fountain, probably brought back by the Rosengartens from Florence, Italy, in the 1920s and originally on the Chanticleer Terraces, is the focal point of a design that replaced a lawn. The Potting Shed, near the Cut Flower Garden, which is used for potting and storage, looks much the same as it did when the garden was opened to the public, but now has rot-resistant siding and a new cedar roof. The nearby cold frames were slated for removal, but thanks to horticulturist Doug Croft's woodworking skills, they feature new masonry and sashes, and gardeners once again vie to use the space.

The biggest structural change was created by taking down Adolph Jr.'s Minder House to build the Ruin. The Ruin is what is called a "folly," built simply for aesthetic pleasure and looking as though the original house had fallen into disrepair. Adolph Jr. explicitly stated his parents' home was to be kept as a museum but didn't say anything about his own home. His will left no doubt that the garden was of utmost importance. He himself razed nearby houses to make way for

Drifts of tulips (*Tulipa* 'Pink Impression' and *T.* 'Apeldoorn') throughout the Cut Flower Garden meet the soaring Bell's Woodland springtime display.

future garden expansion, and now his own residence has become a central feature of the garden, a tribute to his vision. He was a connoisseur of trees and shrubs and even wrote an article on ornamental pruning. He would love the way we train rare maples to look like vines climbing the walls, and how the delicate quinces and winter hazels are espaliered to highlight their early spring blooms.

CHANTICLEER RUNS MUCH LIKE A PRIVATE GARDEN

Chanticleer has seven horticulturists (or gardeners; we use the terms interchangeably). Each is responsible for designing, planting, and maintaining an area of the garden. They are part of a fourteen-person, full-time, year-round horticultural staff. Everyone does winter projects when the garden is closed, ranging from making furniture to sowing seeds. Key additional members of the team are seasonal groundskeepers, assistant horticulturists, interns, volunteers, and guest gardeners from other organizations, all rotating through the various garden areas.

The Chanticleer staff has a wide variety of backgrounds. Some started gardening early in life, planting vegetables and flowers at their parents' homes, and studied horticulture directly out of high school. Others came to the plant world indirectly, first pursuing anthropology, history, business, or art. They studied horticulture as a second career at a university or at a public garden such as nearby Longwood Gardens.

My own path to horticulture was similar to Mr. Rosengarten's. I started gardening when my parents felt their ten-year-old son needed to be constructive with his time. They assigned me the vegetable garden, growing plants that bear produce I previously had refused to eat. I grew bush beans, beets, lettuces (growing a head of iceberg was a goal I never achieved), and tomatoes but not corn, because we were surrounded by fields of sweet corn and our half-acre lot was "too small" for corn. That first season, I carefully followed the instructions on the seed packet, which said to thin the beets and discard. I dutifully discarded. My parents were displeased. They had looked forward to eating the young plants as beet greens. I quickly learned garden "rules" were open to interpretation.

In the process, I discovered that my vegetables were tasty, and I stopped being a picky eater. I began to plant flowers and then roses, using organic gardening techniques. I devoured the two horticultural books in the local library and back issues of the only two periodicals, *Flower Garden* and *Better Homes and Gardens*. I didn't realize there were other gardening magazines or that estates and public gardens existed. Although I didn't grow up on a country estate like Adolph Jr., my midwestern hometown had towering trees and my love and respect for trees grew strong. My parents weren't thrilled when I majored in horticulture at the University of Wisconsin, but luckily, my father disliked law and lawyers even more. The job at Chanticleer is the culmination of my dreams.

In a private garden, the owner makes the decisions. At Chanticleer, the executive director serves as the owner's representative as well as the head gardener, coach, overseer, and benevolent dictator. The board members are closely involved with the garden, giving excellent advice, but they concentrate on policy and finance. The gardeners design, plant, and maintain the garden without an advisory committee and with no long meetings discussing color combinations. This efficient system saves money, avoids bureaucracy, and encourages creativity and good morale. This approach to management may be the biggest single factor in making Chanticleer what it is today.

Each gardener knows her or his area better than anyone else, but may go weeks without visiting the other side of the garden. As leader, I see the entire garden daily, giving me a unique feel for what is essential about the place. We keep the feeling of a private garden, preserving vistas, avoiding signs, and paving as little as possible. We strive to keep the garden looking spectacular every single day. Beds being renovated need to look good for every guest. Hoses still need to be put away when not in use.

Adolph Jr. began each day with a walk around the garden accompanied by his corgi. He greeted the staff, encouraged them to work hard, grabbed a snack at the Apple House, and reviewed the property. I, too, begin each day with a walk around the garden, with my corgi. It's much more than a lovely stroll. It's an inspection tour, a remembrance of what the property was, and most important, a meditation on what it can be.

I stop frequently, looking both up close and into the distance. What does this part of the garden look like to a first-time guest? Is it as good as it can be? How will the area look in a month? In three months? A year? In a decade? Could this bed be better? Is it time to try something new? Should this path be moved? Is that tree going to block the view in twenty years? Would a tower draw guests up the Bulb Meadow, the hill above Asian Woods? Can we eliminate steps to improve accessibility? Do all the garden areas hold together as one garden? I also pull a few weeds, clear the spillways, prune an occasional branch, pick up litter, and check the restrooms.

During these daily walks, I meet with as many of the staff as possible. The horticulturists present their ideas, and if we agree, we implement them. If not, we think about it and discuss it more. Most discussions occur in the garden with plenty of hand waving, while more complicated designs are drawn on paper. Garden hoses, flags, ropes, and even sand poured on snow show where new bed edges will be. Always, there are lists of plants.

Stone faces by sculptor Marcia Donahue seem in a state of evening repose at the Ruin Garden.

Following storms, we all assess damage. I usually walk along our creek, called Bell's Run, to see where there was flooding, where we have erosion, and how the volume of water changed the creek. Sometimes the waterway widens, and elsewhere it may be constricted by a newly formed sandbar. We have built up the banks with rocks, organic matter, and plantings to reduce erosion. We're surrounded on three sides by roads, so a great deal of runoff enters the property during heavy rains. Drainage basins capture water coming in from Church Road and from the parking lot. Cisterns hold nearly 50,000 gallons of rainwater for irrigation. Since we're near the top of the watershed, every gallon of water we stow in a storm is a gallon not going to someone's home downstream. We recently exposed a tributary of the creek that was buried in a pipe in the 1930s. Such "daylighting" (or bringing to the surface a creek previously underground) improves the stream's health and reduces flooding. We found frogs and even a salamander living in the stream within the first year of its being aboveground.

There is no shortage of suggestions from others. Do we listen to them? I joke that the best way to ensure something will not be added to the garden is to suggest its addition. But comments are welcomed. They may come from first-time visitors, regular guests, other horticulturists, people interested in art, my close friends, and of course from the board. We take each criticism seriously and listen to what people say, what journalists write, what bloggers comment.

IDEAS ABOUND AT CHANTICLEER FOR YOUR HOME GARDEN

Much of what we do at Chanticleer is easily transferred to the home garden. Not only is the garden filled with ideas and plants you can use at home, but the garden itself is divided into multiple "garden rooms" on a scale similar to residential gardens. The entire property is a demonstration of gardening applicable to eastern North America and beyond.

The Parking Lot Garden is a low-maintenance area. It is not irrigated, and ground covers reduce weeds. The terraces at the houses feature exquisite plantings requiring a great deal of effort. The Tennis Court Garden, the Pond Garden, and the Long Border near the Entrance Pavilion are sunny perennial plantings that offer varying levels of exuberance and have differing maintenance requirements.

Looking for low-water-usage suggestions? Visit the Gravel Garden. Do you have too much water? See the Pond and Creek Gardens. Shade plantings are in the woodlands and native meadows near the Serpentine Garden and the Ruin. We feature native plants in Bell's Woodland and throughout Chanticleer. Containers with plants run the gamut from wet to dry, simple to complex. Some offer an ensemble of many plants and a few feature a single plant. Some of the containers require a great

Inflated seedpods of *Gomphocarpus physocarpus* are a curious sight, but they are fun in the garden and when added to cut flowers in a vase.

Ebullient late summer plantings seem to engulf the Chanticleer House.

are reduced. Garden designs morph over time, with occasional complete makeovers. Even with seasonal changes, we feather new plants in, rather than stripping the entire space to bare soil and replanting. We want the grounds to look spectacular every day. The age we live in considers the more than two-decade existence of Chanticleer Garden to be a long time. Thanks to Adolph Jr.'s vision and generosity, we think in terms of centuries. Chanticleer is a long-term project and should be beautiful and open to guests for centuries to come.

A delicate spring ephemeral, wood anemone (*Thalictrum thalictroides* f. *rosea*) springs forth near Bell's Run.

OPPOSITE *Iris bucharica*, a bulbous iris from central Asia, thrives in the Gravel Garden's free-draining soil.

Corn poppy (*Papaver rhoeas*) and Caradonna blue sage (*Salvia nemorosa* 'Caradonna') are bright touches in the Rock Ledge amidst the fresh early summer vegetation.

DESIGN

A visit to Chanticleer is a journey.

The garden embraces you as you arrive and quickly transports you from the everyday world into a whole new dimension. You start your visit in a small courtyard, where high stucco walls block out the world. A view to the Teacup fountain pulls you in, and suddenly your senses are immersed in the experience. Light changes, vistas open and close, and you become aware of sounds, colors, and textures all designed to engage and delight.

Chanticleer is divided into rooms or areas, each featuring different physical features and microclimates. Each gardener has a philosophy about his/her area, about the overall Chanticleer experience, and about design. Our gardeners meet regularly as a team to ensure the seamless transition from one horticulturist's area of responsibility to another's. During your visit, you find yourself moving from place to place and from experience to experience surrounded by different plants and plantings, yet somehow you are still in the same garden. We use teamwork, design, and plants to make this happen.

Throughout the garden, we take advantage of the natural topography and the individual features of the garden's site. We keep views open but may frame them with trees, such as the view from the Chanticleer House down the Great Lawn. Other areas, including our woodlands, are visually enclosed using plants. We maximize the potential of shaded areas as well as sunny ones, planting what will grow best in each environment.

The houses and other structures serve both as backdrops and integral components of the garden. Every part of the garden is designed to be enjoyed when viewed from inside the buildings as well as to complement the structures' exteriors. We use themes to tie the individual garden areas together as a whole, while working hard to ensure each area retains its own sense of uniqueness.

We design the garden to please us, making the garden personal, unique, and, we hope, pleasing to you. This respect for the landscape, combined with the personal visions and gardening philosophies of the horticulturists, give the garden "soul." The garden is closely in tune with its surroundings and is a reflection of the individuals who created it.

Our design philosophy can be summarized like this:

Make the most of a site's features
Integrate the structures and the garden
Have themes that tie the areas together into one garden
Change evolutionarily rather than with grand landscape designs
Focus on plants

THE SITE SHAPES OUR DESIGNS

It is easy to love the Chanticleer site, with its 48 acres of rolling hillside, large trees, and meandering creek. The Chanticleer House stands majestically over a long, pastoral view sloping downward to the west. The Rosengartens kept the vista open and unobstructed. We follow suit by maintaining a long, uninterrupted swath of grass, and use adjacent plantings and beds to guide your attention toward the Pond Garden, Serpentine Garden, and woods. This rolling topography is typical of our part of the Pennsylvania Piedmont region, where the land drops to the coastal plain. We use organic methods to keep the turf healthy, and we make sure nothing is planted to block this view. From the rocking chairs outside the house, guests can see how big the property is and catch glimpses of areas inviting exploration. (The entire property measures 48 acres, but the public garden is 35; the remainder is in agricultural fields, service areas, and some staff housing.)

Microclimates Offer Opportunities

There are multiple microclimates within Chanticleer's site. Any outdoor space, be it large, small, or even a balcony, has one or more spots where the growing conditions differ from the rest. All professional and amateur gardeners learn through experience and observation of the varying conditions of their gardens. The most evident microclimates are around buildings. The south side of a structure is warmer and brighter than the north side; the west side is hotter than the east; this is the case around the two houses at Chanticleer. We grow heat-loving plants and marginally hardy ones on the south-facing terraces. The Great Lawn below the main house faces west and experiences strong afternoon light, while much of the rest of the garden is on a north-facing slope. These exposures affect what we plant as well as the quality of light in the various garden rooms. As artists know, light from the north is bright, indirect, bluer, and casts softer shadows.

Winter is an excellent time to study a garden's microclimates. We've observed, for example, that snow melts first on the terraces of the two houses, in the Gravel Garden, and along the Winter Shrub Border, which borders the Great Lawn and features winter bloomers. These warmer areas are great places for winter-blooming plants. A blossom in winter is worth hundreds in spring. The south-facing terraces trap heat, allowing us to push our hardiness zone (USDA Zone 7a) at least to a warmer 7b and sometimes to 8. These places are good ones for borderline hardy plants in winter. During the summer, here we use tropical and subtropical plants that thrive in the heat, and these south-facing terraces are late to be hit by frost.

Snow melts slowly on the north side of the buildings, the north-facing Wildflower Slope, near the Apple House (which is shaded by evergreens to the south), and even on the Bog near the Ponds. This explains why our sun- and heat-loving pitcher plants in the Bog have not thrived as we hoped they would. On the other hand, a heat-intolerant paper birch thrives on the cool soil of the Wildflower Slope as do trilliums and native azaleas.

Soil variation also affects plantings. The Gravel Garden is on a sunny, dry, southwest-facing slope. We've dug gravel into the soil to increase the drainage and make it a drier site. This is our xerophytic site, needing no additional water and allowing us to mimic some California gardens. Lavenders, thymes, yuccas, and butterfly weeds flourish. On the other hand, Adolph Jr. created a pond by digging out a

In a south-facing corner of the Teacup Garden, Japanese banana (*Musa basjoo*) has reliably overwintered with little or no protection for twenty years, underscoring the significance of microclimates.

TOP   Southwest-facing and sunbaked, the Gravel Garden is a xerophytic site. We've amended the soil with gravel to increase drainage, benefitting dry-loving plants.

BOTTOM   Mediterranean plants, like this hybrid lavender (*Lavandula ×intermedia* 'Grosso'), thrive in the Gravel Garden's sunshine and well-drained soil.

Snow melts slowly in the northern exposure of the Bog by the Ponds, indicating a cooler microclimate.

wet area in the 1970s, siphoning water from the creek to supplement the natural springs. We added more ponds in the 1990s, and, taking advantage of the wetter soil, this area is home to our water and bog plants. Similarly, near the Waterwheel, the edges of the underground tributary we brought to the surface have become great places for plants that thrive in moist soil.

Light and shade impact plantings. The humid shade in Bell's Woodland and Asian Woods makes the areas inhospitable for turf but ideal for native and exotic woodland plants. By working with our site rather than fighting it, we treat these microclimates as opportunities rather than problems. As Joe Henderson says, "Make the most of what you've got and don't worry about what you don't have."

Butterfly milkweed (*Asclepias tuberosa*), a tuberous-rooted native perennial, withstands the hot, dry conditions of the Gravel Garden with aplomb.

Paper birch (*Betula papyrifera*) flourishes with sedges and ferns in the cool and moist oasis of the Moss Walk.

Garden Rooms

A garden by definition is an enclosed space. All of Chanticleer is enclosed (by a deer fence, trees, and shrubs), and is further divided into garden rooms. Dividing the larger garden into parts provides the element of surprise for guests, since the whole is not seen all at once, and it also makes the garden feel bigger. Home gardeners relate well to Chanticleer because these "bite-sized" pieces are on a home garden scale and offer a great variety of environments and design concepts.

A good example of a garden room is the Sun Porch on the western side of the Chanticleer House. It once had glass windows and was functionally part of the house itself, extending the house into the garden and the garden into the house. Now, with the windows removed, it is an open-air room. Windowsills hold changing displays of plants, ranging from succulents to ferns to rare bulbs; flowers float in the pot next to the fireplace. Fragrances from the garden drift in, and you feel both inside and out. The Terraces around the house are divided into spaces, and the Ruin continues the concept. Stone walls are covered with vines and espaliered trees and shrubs. Additional walls are formed

by columnar Japanese hollies and plum yews. As one leaves the Ruin, stone furniture beckons, lightly enclosed by encircling trees.

Other rooms include the Pond Arbor, with a ceiling of wisterias and weeping flowering cherries, and wide "windows" opening to the Ponds. The Creek Garden is huge, feeling like a ballroom, with walls of trees on all sides. A large opening at the Waterwheel looks up to the Ruin. The Teacup Garden is a more intimate room, with the Tennis Court slightly larger, walled by shrubs and an arbor.

LEFT   Once an enclosed part of the Chanticleer House, the Sun Porch is an open-air room transitioning between the garden and the house. It is enhanced with garden scents, containers, and cut flowers.

RIGHT   A cathedral-like circle of trees forms a high-ceiling room near the Ruin. Amazingly comfortable stone couches attract guests for group photographs.

With its high-backed, thronelike chairs, wide windowlike vistas, and overhead wisterias and weeping flowering cherries, the Pond Arbor has a regal quality humbled by its rustic materials, stone and weathered wood.

INTEGRATING STRUCTURES AND THE GARDEN

When designing a home garden, it's essential to relate the house to its surroundings. People spend much of their time indoors, and so you should remember to design your garden to be viewed from inside the house as well as outside. Bring the garden into the house with compelling views through windows. Since Chanticleer is not actually a home garden, we use various ways to relate the buildings to the garden. The mood of the Sun Porch is intentionally similar to that of the main house, although the materials differ. Whereas in the main house the fireplace mantles are graced with a clock, candlesticks, or other family items, the Sun Porch's mantle may be festooned with orchids or with a seasonally planted vignette.

Another way we integrate the buildings and garden is by using cut flowers. We bring flowers from the garden to the reception desk, restrooms, and into the Chanticleer House. Flowers brought in from the garden reflect the season and are more personal than purchased flowers. A small porcelain vase of late-winter snowdrops allows for close-up inspection of the delicate green markings on the lovely white petals. We may use a different cultivar of narcissus in each room. Later, the simple beauty of a flowering cherry branch is striking when backlit by the breakfast room window. Sequential spring selections follow, such as tulips, then peonies, irises, and eventually lilies.

High summer is a leafier time in the garden. While there is always something in bloom, we simplify the arrangements. Clear glass vases lined with bold foliage of hostas or elephant ears may hold simple bunches of hydrangeas and ornamental grasses. A few giant leaves in a handmade vase may be all that is needed to brighten the dining room. These arrangements do more than just connect the house to the garden; they bring the rooms to life and add an element of organic softness. We want the fresh flowers in every room to make you feel like it is all done just for you, because it is.

Like a room in the house, the Sun Porch is fully furnished and decorated, in this case with begonias (including the large-leafed 'Lotusland'), ferns, and a large centerpiece of cut flowers floating in a ceramic vessel.

Reflected in a gold-framed mirror, a floral arrangement of *Ageratum houstonianum*, *Cirsium japonicum*, *Dahlia* 'Blue Bell', *Eryngium amethystinum*, and *Eustoma grandiflorum* 'Mariachi Sapphire Blue Chip' brings the highlights of late summer into the foyer of Chanticleer House.

Backlit by the evening light, the uncurling croziers of Dixie wood fern (*Dryopteris ×australis*) and the chalicelike *Tulipa* 'White Triumphator' pool at the base of the Ruin Garden 'dining room' window, which frames the young foliage of *Acer palmatum* 'Bloodgood'.

Contemporary Design Within a Historic Space

JONATHAN WRIGHT

When gardening around the Chanticleer House, I am always aware of its beauty and simplicity. The Terraces are a series of spaces that feel distinct yet open and connected, allowing me to play with plants within a rich framework. The limestone balustrade, now covered with lichens, has only improved with age. I used to wonder what the plantings on the terrace looked like when the Rosengartens were in residence. Chanticleer of today is associated with bold, tropical-themed plant combinations. Would the Rosengartens have enjoyed elephant ears on the terrace? Later, from an old family movie, as the camera scans the back of the house, two things jumped out at me. The first was a potted elephant ears sitting at the base of the steps to the croquet lawn. The second was two large, concrete urns on the terrace flanking the French doors. They had been on the sun porch for as long as I have known Chanticleer, and now I realized they were part of the original terrace.

The main terrace is paved with Vermont slate, streaked with turquoise, matching the roof slate. The slate inspired me to choose silver, purple, and blue-green plants for the container combinations to echo the slate. We have large hanging baskets on the Terraces and their sides (the least attractive part of a basket) are at eye level. To deal with this challenge, we've sometimes woven dogwood and willow stems through the

Original to the estate, the limestone balustrades of the Chanticleer Terraces have acquired a beautiful patina over time from weather and lichens, and admirably enhance the contemporary plantings.

basket to conceal the wire structure, and other times, we've planted the sides so completely that nothing but plants show. One year, to coordinate the baskets with the new flowery lawn in the adjoining terrace, I lined the baskets with living turf, which would grow out through the basket structure, and inserted a few flowers through the basket sides to add to a meadow effect. The basket tops were planted with wiry, see-through plants that would hold their blossoms at eye level. Tulips and cool-season annuals gave way to summer plantings: *Verbena bonariensis*, *Gomphrena* 'Fireworks', *Abutilon* 'Tiber's Red', *Phygelius* 'Purple Prince', *Passiflora* ×*violacea* 'Form #3', *Stachys albotomentosa*, and *Foenicu-*

lum vulgare 'Purpureum' are woven together in this combination. As the season progressed, the turf grass grew, vines climbed upward, and the baskets became wild and airy, a lively contrast to the solid architecture of the house.

The feel of the space alters with the addition or subtraction of a few seasonal plants. One spring, I went for an old-fashioned effect by filling four large pots next to the house with yellow wallflowers, blue Jacob's ladder, silver-leaved centaurea, and trailing rosemary. For height, sweet peas climbed cut willow branches stuck into the center of the pot. For summer, I chose more contemporary selections, replacing the sweet peas with 'Black Thai' banana. The tall,

Unadorned and simple, the Chanticleer Terraces are a series of interconnected spaces extending the house's architecture into the garden.

Current tropical-themed plantings seem contemporary yet actually pay homage to the Chanticleer of yesteryear when the Rosengartens displayed elephant ears (*Colocasia*) in containers.

narrow, blackish stemmed bananas changed the aesthetics of the space instantly. As they grew taller during the season, they guided the eye upward toward the house, connecting the garden and structure.

I had used 'Black Thai' banana the year before at the Teacup Garden in a grid of sixteen plants, which shaded the area by midsummer. Black cotton (*Gossypium herbaceum* 'Nigra'), 'Black Patent Leather' coleus, chocolate cosmos (*Cosmos atrosanguineus*), and black sweet potato vine enhanced the black theme, while silver-leaved *Centaurea cineraria* 'Colchester White', *Euphorbia hypericifolia* 'Diamond Frost', and *Gladiolus murielae* added bright contrast. The gladiolus is sweetly fragrant and its white

blossoms have purple-black markings in the center, the same shade of purple as the banana trunks.

Banana plants can be overwintered easily in a cool basement. Dig the plants just before frost, cut them about 3 feet above the ground to reduce weight, shake off as much soil as possible, and put the roots in a black plastic bag. Leave all winter without watering. In spring, after danger of frost is past, cut off any growth that has occurred in the winter (which will just burn when put outside), and plant outside. It will take about three weeks before enough new growth appears and the plant looks good, so another option is to pot the plants and let them grow first in a "behind the scenes" area.

TOP   Hanging baskets of rose-gray rosettes of *Echeveria* 'Perle Von Nürnberg' and pink spikes of *Agastache* 'Acapulco Salmon & Pink' subtly echo the colors in the Vermont slate paving of Chanticleer Terraces.

BOTTOM   Bananas, such as this *Ensete ventricosum* 'Maurelli' erupting from a coleus (*Plectranthus scutellarioides* 'Rustic Orange'), overwinter well in the cellar.

TOP   Wild and loose, this hanging basket on the Chanticleer Terrace resembles a stylized meadow suspended midair, packed with *Foeniculum vulgare* 'Purpureum', *Gomphrena* 'Fireworks', *Origanum vulgare* 'Aureum', *Passiflora ×violacea* 'Form #3', and *Stachys albotomentosa*.

BOTTOM   The deep color of black cotton (*Gossypium herbaceum* 'Nigra') reinforces a black theme in the Teacup Garden.

A theme of red tones underpins the contemporary planting scheme at the Chanticleer House Overlook. *Cordyline australis* 'Red Sensation' anchors the monochrome mix of *Dahlia* 'Madame Simone Stappers', *D.* 'Verrone's Obsidian', *Plectranthus scutellarioides* 'Redhead', and *Salvia confertiflora*. A potted oxblood lily (*Rhodophiala bifida*) connects the Overlook plantings to the Sun Porch.

Fitting Structures into the Garden

We build structures to complement the garden. We usually involve a team, as we do with any garden project. Facilities manager Ed Hincken and assistant facilities manager Bryan Christ lead and collaborate with a team of contractors and horticulture staff. The process used in designing and building the Asian Woods Restrooms is a good example of our collaborative and creative efforts. The building needed to include toilets, sinks, a covered area to wait out storms, and we wanted the structure to have an Asian quality. Ed Hincken and Lisa Roper went to Japan to study gardens and architecture, with a Japanese horticulturist as their guide. Upon their return, we completed the overall design to resemble a Japanese teahouse. When we poured the concrete floor, falling autumn leaves accumulated on the surface. We blew them off so we could acid stain the floor a dark brown. To our surprise and delight, afterimages of the leaves appeared in the stained surface.

We added more Japanese touches to the structure. We laid a double row of asphalt roof shingles to mimic traditional (and more expensive) Japanese ceramic tiles. Material for a proposed knee wall was changed from stucco to stone, and stone bases were added to the posts. Lisa split and placed a large stepping-stone at the entrance and designed a bamboo screen to shield the service area; Dan Benarcik built the screen. Craftsman Douglas Randolph designed and built benches for the patio. Final accessorizing was done with Lisa's black and white photos and Doug Croft's ceramics.

The Pond Arbor was first built in the 1990s using old barn beams, effectively incorporating an awkward stone wall into the garden. Within a decade, the beams were rotting, endangering the structure. Joe Henderson suggested replacing the vertical supports with round stone columns, which would give the structure long life, and topping them with large white oak beams. Because round columns would need to be wide and would be visually out of proportion, and square seemed too blocky, tapering square columns were chosen as a compromise. A stonemason chose five of the nine types of stone used in the retaining wall behind the arbor. Joe unwound the decade-old wisteria vines from the wood posts, carefully wrapped them, and laid them on the ground. When the mason finished, Joe unwrapped the vines and wound them around the new columns. They bloomed beautifully the following spring.

In designing an Entrance Pavilion for Chanticleer, we wanted to incorporate the look of the surrounding garden and house as well as complement Chanticleer's long-standing tradition of hospitality. The goal was to build a structure that looked like it had always been there, while creating an intimate space where visitors were not separated from our receptionists. We chose a location across from the front door of the house between existing stone pillars and designed a simple structure that mirrored the triangular, tiled rooflines of the house, making

Entwined with *Wisteria floribunda* 'Shiro Noda' and buttressed by handsome stone pillars holding crossbeams, the Pond Arbor visually connects the patio with the garden.

TOP By no means an exact replica of a Japanese teahouse, the Asian Woods Restrooms make modern but subtle allusions to Asian architecture through the strong rooflines, shoji-screenlike walls, and bamboo fencing.

RIGHT The Entrance Pavilion sits comfortably among lush vegetation, its roof shingles matching the style and color of Emily's House, the Chanticleer insignia stylized as a weathervane, and latticework posts a counterpoint to the house's cast-iron porch. Open to the outdoors, it graciously welcomes guests and sets the tone for Chanticleer's integrated house and garden.

it appear that the finished Entrance Pavilion was an extension of the house. Matching wrought and cast iron continued the connection with the garden and the house.

THEMES TIE THE AREAS TOGETHER INTO ONE GARDEN

The Chanticleer experience is like a three-dimensional symphony, with various movements and sections, some vibrant, some quiet, all fitting together as one piece, integrated by themes running through it.

Our basic template is the master plan commissioned by Adolph Jr. in the 1980s, incorporating the houses and gardens on the property together as one. He commissioned local landscape architects Rodney Robinson and Mara Baird to draw up a master plan for the public garden to include a path throughout the acreage and a parking lot. The lot's brown paving and Belgian block edging repeat through the garden. The path curves and weaves, pulling the garden together. Sometimes the path serves as a border between areas, but more often it moves through areas. Edges of the lawn are important in helping to establish the visual flow of the spaces, holding them together and leading you (and your eye) from one spot to another. Bed edges are usually curving, echoing the pathway and the Serpentine Garden. Themes are repeated throughout the garden to unite the whole. The various areas have different names, but they are all part of the overall design. We also use patterns, textures, and physical features to tie the garden together.

Patterns are repeated throughout the garden. You'll find circles in lawn areas, in the path, and in cobblestone edging in the lawn (especially near the Ruin). We repeat textures by laying tiles and stones vertically to create side paths. Gardeners blend transition zones between their areas to ensure uninterrupted flow of plantings, mood, energy, and composition. Each area may echo the plants from the adjacent area in different compositions. Or they may repeat textures and colors with different plants. We hope you and our other guests cannot tell where one horticulturist's area ends and another's begins.

Raked Gravel Circle

Fiddlehead Path

Curving patterns converge and lend symphonic harmony to Chanticleer's diverse garden areas: the
Chanticleer House Gravel Circle raked in concentric circles; blue camassias outlining the curvaceous

Camassia along Bell's Run

Winter Rye at the Serpentine

contours of the creek; the tiled pathway mimics an unfurling fiddlehead fern, hence its name
Fiddlehead Path; and the swooping winter rye at the Serpentine Garden.

Transitions

JOE HENDERSON

As you move through various garden areas, you have a virtual conversation with the Chanticleer gardeners' work through your responses. We create spaces to stand on their own merit as well as work in conjunction with adjacent areas. For example, a glade of dogwoods welcomes you to Asian Woods from the sunny slope of the Serpentine. These trees are Rutgers University hybrids of American flowering dogwoods, *Cornus florida* and *C. nuttallii*, plus the Asian *C. kousa*. You might not think much of them other than that they are pretty trees, but they introduce the first Asian note in the garden as you follow the path. Asian Woods combines a canopy of native hardwood tree species with an understory of exotic Asian flora. The dogwoods provide a mid-canopy transitional device, introducing the woods and serving as a connection between the American and the Asian.

Leaving the controlled docility of the woods, you pass through a dense wall of cryptomerias. A sliver of light exposes a view toward the bright wildness of the Ponds. Once past the Ponds, you are again enveloped in the cool shadows of a mature forest canopy, but instead of Asian plants, you are met with sweeps of native, ground-covering phlox planted in small drifts. Moving about Chanticleer, you are met with many such transitions, mostly subtle moments easily overlooked. These transitions add complexity and a deeper appreciation of the garden.

Repeating plants tie one garden area to another, as these grasses and giant hyssop (*Agastache rupestris*) introduce the Gravel Garden in the beds adjacent to the Ruin.

Cryptomeria japonica 'Yoshino' cordons off Asian Woods from the Pond Garden, emphasizing contrasting light levels and heightening a sense of expectation. Horticulturist Przemek Walczak built the bridge.

Uniting Asian Woods with a Bamboo Theme

LISA ROPER

Bamboo has supple, graceful qualities that fulfill decorative and functional needs.

TOP Faux bamboo culms of flanged copper pipes cover steel bars, providing durable support for the bridge railing in Asian Woods.

We use bamboo as a recurring theme in Asian Woods, unifying the area within and distinguishing it from the rest of Chanticleer. A large grove of *Phyllostachys aureosulcata* inspired me with its elegant, upright green and yellow culms (stems). The straight stems are interrupted by intermittent nodes and an occasional knee-like joint. They create an elegant pattern in the woods, as do their slender, olive-green leaves, which rustle in a breeze. Cut culms edge the secondary paths and are part of the fence adjacent to the restrooms. Bamboo is also used as a design element in a copper bridge railing and in the decorative painting on two Adirondack chairs in the area.

The path edging defines the space in the spring when plants are emerging, and creates a physical barrier to treading on the new shoots. The edging has gone through a few permutations in the past decade. When I first became the Asian Woods gardener, large walnut branches lying on the ground served as edging, but these decayed quickly. Rope was the next delineation, before we moved on to bamboo cane edging.

Bamboo is used in Asia as a renewable building material, and our grove provides a continuing supply for edging. I use large, 2-inch culms of bamboo for the uprights, sleeved over rebar hammered 2 feet into the ground. Oval holes in the tops of the bamboo allow a 1-inch-diameter bamboo culm to be horizontally inserted, connecting the posts. Finally, I tie a Japanese-style knot of black palm rope around the overlapping horizontals, adding stability and ornament.

Split bamboo hoops form temporary edging and low fencing throughout Chanticleer. They are indispensable in preventing people from taking a shortcut through a garden bed or even to mark where the grounds crew should mow a path through the bulb beds. We use a Japanese cast-iron bamboo splitter to cut a bamboo cane into strips. Although these hoops only last a season or two, they are easily reproduced using our own bamboo.

Bamboo cane edging protects plants from wandering feet and distinguishes Asian Woods from other areas of Chanticleer.

LEFT Split bamboo hoops, which we make from our own bamboo, are simple, attractive, temporary edging and fencing.

EVOLUTIONARY CHANGE RATHER THAN GRAND LANDSCAPE DESIGNS

A landscape design is usually something installed at one time and expected to remain essentially the same. A garden evolves over time, from season to season, year to year, decade to decade. Both Bell's Woodland and Asian Woods slowly transitioned from weedy wooded areas into woodland gardens. Each took nearly a decade before they became significant garden features. There is change through the seasons, with major colors evolving from season to season. Winter and early spring tend to be white and yellow. The colors gradually move into a period of reds and purples in late spring, later to yellows and oranges of summer, and finally purples, reds, and yellows of autumn. Winter is a visually open time and many garden areas are flat, with their herbaceous plants cut to the ground. The Pond area exemplifies this progression. In winter and spring, the area is flat and open. By early summer, the area is much more enclosed, and by late summer it feels almost like a secret garden. As leaves drop in the cool weather of autumn, the area gradually becomes more open again.

Evolution means constant refining, adding and removing plants and changing bed edges. In our case, we often add more of a curve to a bed or extend it out as a tree or shrub gets larger, uniting two or more beds as they gradually enlarge.

Beauty persists in the autumnal Pond Garden.

Transitioning from Spring into Summer

JONATHAN WRIGHT

No area of our garden can afford to have a downtime; guests do not come to see bare ground. The terraces of the two houses go through two major plantings each year: one in the spring and one for the summer and autumn. We could rip out the spring planting all at once and then replant for the summer, which is simple, allows the soil to be worked, and avoids tiptoeing around existing plantings. But because that approach leaves beds empty for several days and the new plants are small, we instead gradually take out the spring display, replacing it with the summer planting. In this way, the seasonal transitions are so smooth our guests hardly know they're seeing a changeover.

I pull cool-season plants as they fade and replace them with heat-loving plants, a little at a time. A consistent color scheme through the seasons makes this easier. For example, on the Chanticleer Terraces, I fall-planted a mixture of three kinds of yellow tulips with early, mid, and late bloom times, spaced about 12 to 14 inches apart. For contrast, I added 'Black Parrot' tulips for a polka-dot effect. As the tulips emerged, I planted bronze fennel between the emerging dark tulips. Between the yellow ones, I planted lavender wallflowers and sweet alyssums in shades of purple and lavender. The wallflowers and alyssum added color before and while the tulips bloomed in mid-spring. The yellow tulips looked spectacular with lavender blooms at their toes, and continued a display for quite some time because of the staggered bloom time of the three cultivars. As the yellow tulips peaked, the 'Black Parrot' tulips opened above the ferny mist of the bronze fennel foliage. After heavy rains knocked the last of the yellow tulip petals to the ground, we carefully pulled the tulips from the soft soil. The remaining ground cover of lilac-colored blooms was accented

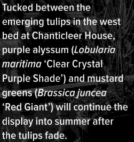

Tucked between the emerging tulips in the west bed at Chanticleer House, purple alyssum (*Lobularia maritima* 'Clear Crystal Purple Shade') and mustard greens (*Brassica juncea* 'Red Giant') will continue the display into summer after the tulips fade.

with clusters of 'Black Parrot' tulips and bronze fennel.

As the black tulips dropped their petals and were pulled, I inserted summer plants among the alyssum and wallflowers. I continued the purple color scheme with *Strobilanthes dyerianus*, *Verbena bonariensis*, *Capsicum annuum* 'Black Pearl', *Heliotropium arborescens* 'Scentropia Dark Blue', and *Salvia splendens* 'Paul'. *Centaurea cineraria* 'Colchester White' and *Silybum marianum* added silver; green-flowering *Nicotiana langsdorffii* and *Abutilon* 'Tangerine' accented it all. The planting always felt established and filled in, with consistent color and textural themes that worked together. In another bed, spring-planted burgundy lettuces, kale, mustard greens, and beets were slowly harvested over time, and replaced with burgundy coleus, hemigraphis, and *Alternanthera* cultivars.

A similar, gradual changeover was done in containers with a burgundy and red theme. In early spring, I sank 12-inch pots of red tulips into the center of each container, hiding the pot edges with compost. The fall-planted bulbs spent the winter in unheated cold frames. To provide color before the tulips bloomed, I surrounded the bulb pots with *Heuchera* 'Frosted Violet', *Foeniculum vulgare* 'Purpureum', *Erysimum cheiri* 'Blood Red', *Ranunculus asiaticus* 'La Belle' (red), and *Salvia officinalis* 'Purpurascens'. Cut stems of red-twigged dogwood supported the wallflowers (*Erysimum*) and continued the red theme, adding colorful height. After blooming, I deadheaded the tulips and removed the spent ranunculus bulbs, their places easily concealed by the expanded heuchera foliage. The wallflowers took center stage. I lifted the pot of faded tulips and planted a burgundy-leaved crinum. A few weeks later when the hot weather arrived, I removed the bronze fennel, purple sage, and wallflowers and filled the openings with *Elegia tectorum*, *Aeonium* 'Plum Purdy', *Begonia boliviensis* 'Bonfire', *Russelia* 'St. Elmo's Fire', and a trailing, narrow-leaved *Hemigraphis repanda*.

Permanent players like *Euphorbia amygdaloides* 'Ruby Glow', *Heuchera* 'Marmalade', and *Salix alba* var. *sericea* ensure a seamless summer changeover after salmon *Tulipa* 'Menton' and purple lily-flowered *Tulipa* 'Maytime' have finished their season in the Teacup Garden.

SPECIFIC DESIGN EXAMPLES

The horticulturists take the lead on designing their garden areas. Each area is unique and each person has a different aesthetic outlook. Here, several of our staff discuss their approaches to design.

The orange torches of red-hot poker (*Kniphofia* 'Shining Spectre') playfully cut through indigo woodland sage (*Salvia forsskaolii*) at the Rock Ledge.

Creating a New Bed and Pathway

JOE HENDERSON

Designs usually start off as solutions to problems. A steep, turfed hillside between the Gravel Garden and the Ponds was too steep for safe walking or mowing and was bordered with liriope on one side and a mixed bed (the Rock Ledge) on the other. The top of the slope had good views to the Ponds and to the Bulb Meadow in the distance. Extending the Rock Ledge across the slope would hide the path, immerse the participant in color, and a switchback would conquer the steepness. Inspired by the architecture of a Greek amphitheater, granite seats would double as steps, sweeping down to the stage (the Ponds). I laid out the new path with marking flags, walked it repeatedly, and got input from colleagues.

I moved granite steps from the Pond Arbor to continue the Gravel Garden steps and provide seating for the amphitheater. The pace slows with the grade, allowing you to see flower structure from below and color from above. From a distance, all you see is a large flower bed. We used an AIR-SPADE to dig the established liriope, carving blocks of plants for easy transport. Liriope is not a favorite of us plant snobs, but it is a tough plant, and it now slows storm water flowing from the road above the Serpentine. We laid the clumps on bare soil and filled in with compost. The clumps rooted well and thrive in the new shaded location, just as they previously prospered in full sun.

This photo shows the Rock Ledge before it was expanded across the hill. The change eliminated an unsafe steep lawn and created a magical walkway through a cascade of color.

The expanded Rock Ledge, with granite steps, is partially obscured by self-sown *Leucanthemum vulgare*, *Orlaya grandiflora*, and *Papaver rhoeas* accented with perennial *Salvia nemerosa* 'Caradonna' that flow downward from the Gravel Garden and to the Ponds.

Ribbons of Grasses as a Unifying Element

JONATHAN WRIGHT

My design for the Tennis Court Garden is meant to be viewed from the landing at the top of the stairs, the "picture spot." The Tennis Court consists of five rectangular beds divided by lawn paths. I thought of the five beds as one, ignoring the paths, and wove long, narrow bands of grasslike plants throughout the space to give visual movement, as if the plants were jumping across the paths. I used grasses (*Panicum virgatum* 'Shenandoah' and *Calamagrostis ×acutiflora* 'Karl Foerster') plus grasslike *Iris sibirica* 'Dancing Nanou' (with purple-blue blossoms) and *Kniphofia* 'Alcazar' (orange blossoms after the irises). With the ribbons connecting the five beds, I added other perennials and bulbs, also repeated across the beds. Tulips emerge, bloom, and fade, then later, perennials fill in. A mix of hundreds of ornamental onions (*Allium* 'Globemaster,' *A.* 'Summer Drummer,' *A.* 'Ambassador,' *A.* 'Mars,' *A.* 'Gladiator,' *A.* 'Purple Sensation', and *A. giganteum*) bloom from late spring into early summer.

The grassy ribbons function like hedges, with the spaces in between becoming pockets to try new plant combinations. These spaces also are opportunities to interject smaller numbers of plants and allow for discovery. I echoed the blood red veins on orange abutilon's petals with a deep red-flowered *Salvia splendens* 'Van-Houttei' and contrasted them with the burgundy foliage of *Iresine* at their feet.

Grassy ribbons of *Panicum virgatum* 'Shenandoah' and *Calamagrostis ×acutiflora* 'Karl Foerster' unite the Tennis Court's beds. These ribbons provide enclosure, lessen the formality of this garden room, and create opportunities to highlight small groupings of plants, or vignettes, within the partitions.

Designing the Teacup Garden: Two Approaches

Horticulturists Jonathan Wright and Dan Benarcik designed the Teacup Garden in succeeding years. Each chose a very different yet successful theme for the space. Here is how they describe their designs.

Dan Benarcik's design for the Teacup Garden features the boldness of orange, tempered with contrasting tones.

Designing with Cool Silvery Blue

JONATHAN WRIGHT

I wanted the normally hot, south-facing Teacup Garden visually to feel cooler and calming. I chose a desert theme centered on massive specimens of *Agave americana*. I have a soft spot for hard-looking plants, and the silvery blue of these agaves worked perfectly. The agaves' forms would imitate fountains, rising from a "pool" of silver blue foliage, and would surround an actual fountain, the Teacup.

What plants could help me create this effect? A simple, silvery blue carpet of one type of plant could give good effect but would be visually dull upon closer inspection. Instead, I chose a variety of plants for their low-growing habit and silvery aspect. Silver-leaved *Dichondra argentea* crept on the ground and filled in between *Salvia chamaedryoides*, *Oxypetalum caeruleum*, and *Salvia sinaloensis*. To accent the carpet-like plants, numerous small agaves were tucked in randomly, replicating the large agaves in a diminutive scale. A bonus, the burgundy-blushed foliage of sinaloa sage picked up on the color of the spines on the emerging agave leaves.

The silvery blues of *Agave americana* (lower right) and *Bismarckia nobilis* (upper left) along with the flowers of *Salvia sinaloensis* dial down the heat of the south-facing Teacup Garden.

Designing with Hot Orange

DAN BENARCIK

Orange is bright and confident, but can be jarring if not balanced with contrasting colors. I started the season with orange-flowered tulips (*Tulipa* 'Fire Wings' and *T.* 'Orange Princess') in clusters of four to six, spaced roughly 18 to 24 inches apart, marking each cluster with a stick. I did not mix the cultivars, so the different bloom times created pools of color at various times in different places. In mid-winter, I moved *Salix alba* var. *sericea* into the square planting bed around the Teacup fountain. I enjoy the willow's olivelike form and cool, silvery foliage, and I added potted olives once the chance of frost was past. By siting the real near the imposter, I hoped to give the impression that all the trees were olives, a bit of Tuscany in Pennsylvania.

I reinforced the orange-flowering bulbs with *Diascia* 'Flirtation Orange', *Osteospermum* 'Serenity Bronze', and *Geum* 'Totally Tangerine' for height, plus *Heuchera* 'Caramel' for mass and weight. We filled lingering gaps with 'Champagne Bubbles' Iceland poppies, varying from perky white to orange to red-pink. Perennial *Artemisia* 'Powis Castle' and *Euphorbia* ×*martini* 'Tiny Tim' added to the silver values of

Infusions of burgundy and silver plants temper the brashness of oranges in the Teacup Garden. *Diascia* 'Flirtation Orange' and *Plectranthus scutellarioides* 'Rustic Orange' balance with burgundy spikes of *Ananas comosus* 'Smooth Cayenne', *Phormium tenax* 'Atropurpureum', and *Pennisetum purpureum* 'Vertigo', and are dark foils for *Euphorbia* ×*martini* 'Tiny Tim' and olivelike *Salix alba* var. *sericea*.

the willows. The hardy perennials allowed for a modified version of this bed combination the following year. I inserted frost-tolerant, burgundy brassicas—pak choi (*Brassica rapa* var. *chinensis* 'Violetta'), mustard (*Brassica juncea* 'Red Giant'), and kale (*Brassica napus* var. *pabularia* 'Red Russian')—around the bulbs in contiguous masses (some long and winding, some small and dense). The osteospermums, poppies, and diascias hit their stride as the bulbs faded.

We easily pulled the clustered tulips without disrupting the other plants, creating gaps for a warm-season layer. The brown pineapple 'Cayenne' replaced tulips, followed by a striking orange bromeliad (*Aechmea blanchetiana*), chenille plant (*Acalypha hispida*), large firecracker plant (*Cuphea* 'David Verity'), and Caribbean copper plant (*Euphorbia cotinifolia*).

Dragon's breath (*Hemigraphis repanda*) formed a deep purple carpet. The surrounding beds followed the same color scheme. The design is visually simple, with only three colors—orange, burgundy, and silver. As your eye travels over the Teacup courtyard, you notice a pair of soft orange Adirondack-style chairs in the distance. Four tall, thin, black containers topped with orange bromeliad (*Aechmea blanchetiana*) complete the ensemble.

LEFT   In early autumn, the Teacup Garden still pulsates with burgundy, orange, and silver, and sculptural bromeliads (*Aechmea blanchetiana)* in plinthlike containers resemble ghostly guests in the garden.

RIGHT   The last of the orange blossoms, lion's tail (*Leonotis leonurus*) has striking whorls of tubular flowers appropriately blooming at Halloween if early frosts have not struck.

Building a Design Around a Special Plant

Occasionally, we grow a plant just for its surprise factor. Himalayan blue poppies, *Meconopsis*, for example, are fantasy plants for most gardeners because they cannot withstand temperatures above 80°F for prolonged periods and take three years to grow from seed. They are impractical for Mid-Atlantic gardens, but one Philadelphian brings her *Meconopsis* plants with her to Maine each summer to keep them happy, returning with them in autumn.

We chose another way to avoid our summer heat. We bought mature plants from Alaska in autumn, potted them in gallon-sized nursery pots, and overwintered them in cold frames. By late winter, each pot contained a beautiful, pubescent rosette of foliage, just ready to send up bloom stalks. The cold frames brought the poppies into bloom a couple of weeks earlier than usual in the spring, and so the plants were able to flower a bit longer before the weather turned hot.

The sky blue poppies (*Meconopsis* 'Lingholm') fueled the design for these spring plantings in the Entrance area. Jonathan Wright chose a matrix of soft grass studded with yellow flowers to contrast with the blue poppies. *Osteospermum*, *Nemesia*, *Narcissus*, and *Erysimum* flowered yellow surrounded by the golden grassy foliage of *Carex elata* 'Bowles's Golden' and the soft, fresh green of Mexican feather grass (*Nassella tenuissima*) weaving the planting together. *Lathyrus sativus* added more clear blue, climbing on yellow twig dogwood branches stuck into the ground. The branches were arranged to resemble living dogwoods (and some actually rooted and started growing). The peas climbed up through the twigs, softening the bare stems of the twigs while the blooms echoed the color of the poppies. We enjoyed the extravagance for several springs, buying new poppies each autumn.

Mid-Atlantic gardeners covet Himalayan blue poppies (*Meconopsis* 'Lingholm') for their clear blooms worthy of extreme efforts.

Container Culture

DAN BENARCIK

Container display is the control freak's ultimate power trip. You choose the vessel, the plants, soil mix, watering and fertilization schedule, and location. The smaller soil mass in a container heats earlier in the season than garden soil, and manipulating the drainage and soil mix allows for horticultural theatrics. Pots can be moved from a situation of optimal light to temporarily enliven another area. Emptied pots store easily in dry or frost-free areas for the winter and can move to a different location the following year. Containers are a great place to try out plant combinations and to allow a young tree or shrub to grow to a larger landscape size.

I fill the bottom two-thirds of a container with compost, including sticks, stones, and worms. This bottom layer lends major nutrients, micro-nutrients, and moisture-holding capacity. I fill the rest of the pot with a commercial potting mix. Such a mix encourages root development of young plants early in the season. These young roots wouldn't stand a chance in the heavy compost or garden soil. As the season progresses, the roots work their way down to the compost, tapping into the reserves of nutrients and moisture. The weight of the bottom layer is ballast for the container, reducing the chance of falling over from incidental bumping or strong wind.

Containers can range from a spectacular vessel as the showpiece in a courtyard to a series of similarly planted pots screening a view. Bigger is better in terms of plants, plantings, and containers. Dark containers heat up in the sun for early warmth in the spring. In the summer heat, I move them to shaded locations or cover them with vines or sprawlers. Handmade, wooden,

Besides allowing for unconventional combinations, grouping containers can enliven entryways as they do near the Entrance Pavilion patio.

Repetition can increase the visual power of containers. A trio of olive (*Olea europaea* 'Arbequina') and million bells (*Calibrachoa* 'MiniFamous Compact Orange') offers immediate impact at the Entrance Pavilion.

L-shaped "pot feet" create an air space below the pot, improving drainage, air-pruning roots, and reducing staining of the surface under pots. I wedge three of them under round containers and four under square or irregularly shaped containers.

Unless growing aquatic plants, drainage holes in containers are essential. Large holes big enough to stick a thumb through clog less than smaller ones and can be enlarged or created with a masonry-tipped drill. One year, I wanted to use a large container during the summer for a large tropical aquatic planting, but wanted to first use the pot for a spring planting of annuals. The big bowl had holes 4 inches from the top of the container but none at the bottom. To overcome the drainage issues without drilling a new hole, I cut a disk of scrap plywood just large enough to fit inside the top lip of the pot and small enough to lodge against the sides of the pot just below the height of the drainage hole high on the side of the pot. A single center-

Detailing on containers complements the plants' lines and textures when chosen carefully and kept simple: (opposite) the wavy design on the terra-cotta pot draws your eye to the squiggly leaf margins of *Alocasia* 'Polly' and the scalloped leaves of *Plectranthus scutellarioides* 'Brown Sugar Drop'; (right) the glaze drip pattern emphasizes the large petioles of *Strelitzia alba*; (left) the pot's ebony ribbing captures the smoky moodiness of *Iresine* 'Purple Lady' and *Latania lontaroides* while highlighting *Coprosma repens* 'Tequila Sunrise'.

mounted leg in the middle of the disk rested on the bottom of the pot for additional support. I filled the top 6 inches of the container with potting mix and planted cool-season annuals. In late May, I removed the plants and the disk and replanted with a water-guzzling tropical that appreciated the reservoir of moisture at the bottom of the container.

TOP   Handmade wooden L-shaped "pot feet," like these placed under a pot of succulents, securely lift pots to aerate the undersides.

BOTTOM   A bold bromeliad specimen like *Alcantarea imperialis* can serve as a focal point that injects order in disparate container plantings.

OPPOSITE   Black containers warm up quickly in the spring and can be cooled in the summer with trailing plants, such as *Dichondra argentea* 'Silver Falls' draping below *Aechmea blanchetiana*.

The Evolution of the Gravel Garden

LISA ROPER

The Gravel Garden faces southwest and large granite steps cascade down a gradual slope. We amended the soil with gravel to improve drainage, making a hot and dry location even drier. The area has an attractive wildness to it, yet with a rhythm provided by fine-textured grasses, gray-leafed santolinas, lavenders, milkweed, thyme, and sprawling purple poppy mallow (*Callirhoe involucrata*) that flow throughout. The plants here self-sow, and this randomness, along with repetition of strategically placed plants, creates a naturalistic feeling to the garden. It is its strength but also its challenge. If the wildness gets out of hand, the garden can become a tangle of aggressive plants.

Editing is an integral part of having a "wild" garden. For the garden to feel naturalistic, it should have repetition from aggressive seeders like asters and callirhoe, but I can't let them take over. I also need less aggressive focal points dotted throughout. I spent the first winter dreaming up plans for the Gravel Garden. Ideas included increasing plants that had declined, like giant hyssop (*Agastache rupestris*), with its spikes of dusky orange flowers. It blooms late summer into fall, just when the garden is going through a pre-aster lull. I introduced *Melinis nerviglumis*. This graceful South African grass is a low, blue-green-leafed tender perennial with pink seed heads carried high above the foliage in late summer and fall.

I also wanted to include more bold succulents like agaves, yuccas, and aloes to add texture and form. Grown in our cool greenhouse over

Lavenders, butterfly weeds, thymes, and grasses move with the summertime breezes across the granite steps in the Gravel Garden.

TOP Here, rigorous editing of self-sowers and midsummer pruning especially for asters, *Symphyotrichum oblongifolium* 'October Skies', maintain the balance between simple neutral spaces of gravel and the free-flowing plantings in the Gravel Garden.

BOTTOM Orange geums (*Geum* 'Starkers Magnificum') provide a punch in a rather restrained scene of cool greens and blues (*Festuca idahoensis*, *Lavandula ×intermedia* 'Grosso', *Yucca rostrata*). The geum's color is echoed by California poppies (*Eschscholzia californica*) in the second half of the season.

the winter, these big plants remain in the ground until frosts hit in autumn. I'm experimenting with some of the hardiest succulents, such as *Agave parryi*, hoping they can survive our winters. The problem is not so much cold intolerance as wet soils combined with cold. I'm planting some into mounds of rock and gravel built up above ground level for sharp drainage and providing the plant with a clear cover during the winter to prevent moisture from collecting in the surrounding soil and around the leaves. These techniques might stretch the limits of borderline succulents, allowing them to overwinter in the soil with improved drainage.

The dark, conical *Juniperus virginiana* 'Emerald Sentinel' and spiky *Yucca rostrata* add year-round structure and height amidst the fleeting colors of *Euphorbia epithymoides* and *Tulipa* 'Oratorio' in early spring.

Building Bell's Woodland from Scratch

PRZEMEK WALCZAK

I took over Bell's Woodland seven years before it opened to the public, with the intention of making this peripheral area a native plant garden. Measuring nearly 4 acres, the woodland is on a gentle, south-facing slope, transected by Bell's Run Creek. The woods had mature beeches, oaks, and tuliptrees but had lost one-third of the canopy because of sewer construction, which left a 40-foot-wide stretch of sterile subsoil. Storm water flows in from the nearby road and the creek is flood-prone. The ground layer consisted of some natives but also invasive exotic weeds, including *Euonymus alatus*, *Rhodotypos scandens*, and *Ficaria verna*. Soil remediation, weed eradication, and path location were the first steps in building the new garden.

The permeable main path is wheelchair accessible, built of shredded tires held together by a binder laid on top of the soil to avoid root-damaging excavation. Our respect and under-standing of trees were guiding principles while working on the layout of the area. We lined the route with 6-inch metal edging, added 4 inches of gravel for drainage, and poured 2 inches of the shredded tire material. The secondary path follows Bell's Run and is made of large, heavy stones from central Pennsylvania to withstand periodic flooding. This path is similar to one we saw on a staff outing to Ricketts Glen State Park in central Pennsylvania. Landscape architect Darrel Morrison helped lay out both paths in the woodland.

We took advantage of the topography in locating a bridge to cross the creek. The bridge rises 12 feet above Bell's Run, offering

Through extensive renovation, Bell's Woodland has been given a new identity as a native plant garden, with ferns and mosses, spring ephemerals, and woody plants of eastern North America.

Flat stones were carefully transported and laid for the sturdy path along Bell's Run.

Mosses make excellent seedbeds for self-sowers and, unfortunately, weeds, which need to be vigilantly removed. Here, tiarella seedlings seem happy in the consistently moist, cool conditions of the moss bed while an errant dandelion seedling near the trunk begs to be eradicated.

Eastern redbud (*Cercis canadensis*), one of the first trees to bloom in spring, looks resplendent against the straight tuliptree trunks and fresh spring beech leaves in Bell's Woodland, celebrating the beauty of eastern North American forests.

a distinctive vantage point to the observer. The bridge had three inspirations. One came during a visit to the Pacific Northwest temperate rain forest on Vancouver Island, where the giant, fallen western red cedars fascinated me. Some of them spanned ravines and looked like living bridges as they became nurse logs covered with mosses, ferns, shrubs, and even trees growing up from them. The second inspiration was from cartoons in which logs are used as hiding places from pursuing villains. Such logs are hard to come by so I had to build my own. Third, a hickory had fallen in the woods, turning its circle of roots vertically. It gave us a nearby example to mimic: a long, tubular bridge with a tunnel of circling roots at one end.

Soil remediation was a major undertaking, solved by bringing in a crew of contractual help. We hand-dug together, incorporating compost and woodchips into the previously sterile subsoil. We seeded the area with partridge peas, a native, yellow-flowering annual. Within a year, the peas were replaced by tree, shrub, and wildflower seedlings, including tuliptrees. Bringing the invasive exotic weeds under control was a multiyear process. We continued to hand-dig, spray, and heavily mulch. As the weed population decreased, I planted. Partridge peas again provided quick cover to prevent other weeds from establishing a foothold. Instead of hauling away brush, twigs, and other debris, I built compost

piles throughout the woods, often with a grouping of fallen branches to hold the pile in place. As these piles decompose, they change the soil in the area, creating their own microclimates.

We built upon the natural plant groupings already existing in the area. In some spots, there were groves of beech tree suckers. Intermingling with these were large oaks and beeches, and to the north, a swath of redbuds. The soil varies greatly in the area: in some spots wet and poorly drained, and elsewhere rich and undisturbed. Imposing a design on the area would have resulted in much frustration because plants might do poorly in certain areas. Instead, we put in small groups of plants where they would look good. If they thrived, I added more to supplement the already multiplying plants. If one species didn't succeed, I tried another.

My lifetime love of mosses is easily seen throughout Bell's Woodland. Where mosses naturally occurred, I helped them with hand-weeding. (Don't let anyone tell you mosses are low maintenance.) In other areas, we brought in mosses. At first, we transplanted from other areas of Chanticleer. Later, enthusiastic volunteer John Ryan scouted for available local mosses. When he sees a dilapidated building covered in moss, he asks the owner for permission to scoop off some clumps and brings them to us. His days are spent kneeling, as he lays down the patches of moss like sod.

TOP   From this interior perspective, Bell's Woodland appears to be an appliqued leaf on the bridge's wood-slat surface.

Spanning 60 feet, the Bell's Woodland bridge mimics a fallen tree with splayed roots.

WHAT WE DO IN WINTER

People will ask what we do when the garden is closed in winter because they assume that is downtime for us. Not so. November is one of our busiest months, when we hurry to move tropicals indoors, plant bulbs, rake leaves, winterize pipes, and do construction projects—all with the knowledge that cold weather, frozen soil, and snow are coming. Weather cooperating, this work continues into late autumn. Late winter is also a time of pressure, with a daily countdown till our spring opening.

Two months of winter, January and February, are left as our true wintertime. Even then, we perform horticultural work, including tree and shrub pruning, which is a traditional garden task in these months, when trees and shrubs are slumbering and the sap is not running.

The Role of Arts and Crafts at Chanticleer

Douglas Randolph's idiosyncratic approach to furniture making is conveyed through this carved stone-topped table and leaf-motif carved chairs at Chanticleer House. The leaves of snake plant (*Sansevieria trifasciata*) in the pot on the table cheekily repeat the chairs' irregular contours.

In winter, each gardener has indoor projects, often in our wood and metal shops, where they design and create furniture, gates, bridges, fences, plant list boxes, railings, and drinking fountains. These handmade items give the garden a unique, personalized feeling and add sculpture to the garden although they are not really sculptures per se. Some of the items are unique designs and others are adaptations of what we've seen elsewhere. Our media include wood (often from the property), metal (iron and aluminum), ceramic, and stone.

A face boulder by the sculptor Marcia Donahue looks restful sleeping at the base of the Ruin Meadow.

These winter projects came about serendipitously. Douglas Randolph, one of the first horticulturists hired after Adolph Jr. died, felt underemployed in winter and suggested purchasing woodworking equipment. Douglas built a glider (a rocking bench) for the Tennis Court Arbor and went on to construct some of our finest furniture. When sculptor Marcia Donahue was here in 1999 to carve stone for the Ruin, Douglas studied with her and began carving himself. He helped her carve sculptured stone leaves in the creek and went on to create our drinking fountains, stone tables on the Chanticleer Terraces, and the Ruin's stone furniture.

Dan Benarcik also knew his way around a woodshop and began making furniture. Whereas Douglas liked to dream up a totally unique piece, Dan is intrigued by adapting a design for efficient production. He will see a chair or bench he admires (sometimes at curbside on trash day) and figure out how to make more of them. He has made a name for himself with chair-building workshops with an adaptation of the "Wave Hill" chair, itself inspired by a 1918 chair by Dutch furniture designer and architect Gerrit Rietveld. When Emma Seniuk arrived at Chanticleer, she saw a need for a "serious" workbench for the Potting Shed that would be large enough to mix a wheelbarrow of soil. She turned to Dan and they selected a piece of white oak milled from a fallen tree on the property. After a few days of measuring, cutting, and bonding (of wood and themselves), the two created a beautiful potting bench; it even had collapsible legs, so it could be folded when not in use.

The shape of Lisa Roper's Osage orange bench follows the concave surface of the stone wall on the Asian Woods patio.

OPPOSITE Fashioned from black locust planks, Dan Benarcik's high-backed chairs at the Pond Arbor are minimalist in conception, and their spare lines are clean and rustic against the mosaiclike stonework.

Lisa Roper offers her viewpoint: "Our arts and crafts are utilitarian, designed for function and related to their surroundings. I designed rebar trellises in Asian Woods to look like vines snaking their way around the trunks, blending with the natural environment of the woodland. When a larch tree died, the trunk became a rustic bench. I spent a few weeks in our woodshop teaching myself to build the bench. When I had questions, I turned to Dan Benarcik, Douglas Randolph, and Przemek Walczak. Rustic furniture has an organic form with no straight lines. Fitting it together and gluing it is akin to putting together an intricate puzzle. After completing the bench, chairs and a coffee table followed in successive years. I later made a bench of Osage orange (*Maclura pomifera*), a decay-resistant, incredibly hard wood. The curve of the bench fits on a small patio in Asian Woods overlooking Bell's Run."

Horticulturist Przemek Walczak began making wood bridges and furniture soon after he started work here. Intrigued with metal, he asked to attend a metalworking class. When a new fence was needed around the Waterwheel, he suggested we outfit a garage with used tools and materials "for a small amount of money" for a metal shop. Joe Henderson volunteered to assist, and soon we had two metalworkers and a new fence around the Waterwheel. The fence has a circular motif, inspired by unfurling fern fronds and the Waterwheel itself. They next made a meadow-inspired deer fence at the Chanticleer House driveway. Joe made hand-wrought railings for the Entrance Pavilion and Teacup Garden. Przemek designed and built the Bell's Woodland bridge. Joe describes his love of steel: "Mild steel offers an organic fluidity other materials lack. Inspired by Art Nouveau artists Victor Horta and Josep Jujol, I use techniques not prone to mass production. Otherwise why not just buy it?"

When Emma Seniuk needed a new archway and gate in the Vegetable Garden, Przemek taught her welding and they built the arch. Dan helped with the wooden gate, reusing part of the existing fence. Douglas Randolph instructed Doug Croft on building cold-frame sashes, and together they built the Vegetable Garden bench. Jonathan Wright and horticulturist Terry Struve have learned how to cast leaves in concrete, which sometimes make an appearance in Chanticleer House's Sun Porch and garden beds. Artistry seems to be contagious.

Dan Benarcik finds winter is a time to slow down—to stop, look, and listen to our gardens. He and his colleagues think back to the cues and suggestions from the garden and become inspired by what could happen next year, including identifying seating opportunities derived from the local cues of color, mood, or material. Dan states, "Our furniture is connected to the garden aesthetically and literally. When we lost an ailing white oak, a portable sawyer milled this durable exterior hardwood into usable slabs. Stacked discreetly onsite, it air-dried for two years and is now becoming new chairs and garden experiences. What could better fulfill the circular nature of the garden than to have the chance to sit on an actual extension of the garden itself?"

CLOCKWISE FROM TOP LEFT Doug Croft's glazed ceramic tiles hang in the courtyard of the Asian Woods restrooms.

Unfurling fern fronds inspired Przemek Walczak and Joe Henderson to forge a coiling motif in the Waterwheel fence.

The Vegetable Garden bench delights guests who recognize the carved beets, carrots, and pumpkin.

Sculpture

ABOVE   The dogwood railing connects the Teacup Garden with the Lower Courtyard, showing Joe Henderson's attention to detail, such as the slight folds of the dogwood petals.

OPPOSITE, TOP   After learning carving from the sculptor Marcia Donahue, Douglas Randolph, one of the early horticulturists at Chanticleer, applied his skills to these tree stump pedestals for the bench at the Ruin. He wasn't able to finish them, so stonemason Marty McCabe completed the carving. In the background, the two bald cypresses seem to grow from the bench stumps.

BOTTOM.   Borrowing from Art Nouveau design, Przemek Walczak and Joe Henderson teased steel into sinuous lines on the Chanticleer House fence and gate that organically transform into plant forms.

While Chanticleer is not a sculpture garden, we do have sculpture at the garden. The Rosen-gartens collected lead roosters, installed some ornamental sundials and fountains (including the Teacup fountain), and added several lead sculptures on the Chanticleer Terraces. Adolph Jr. commissioned two stone raccoons by Lyn L. Claytor and a bronze girl by Paul Anthony Greenwood. The raccoons are still in the garden and the bronze girl is at the bottom of the Round Pool near the Waterwheel, an eerie surprise when the water is clear.

When the Ruin was being built, Marcia Dona-hue was our artist-in-residence, carving stone books, leaves, acorns, and faces for the Ruin, as well as leaves in Bell's Run and several faces. Marcia's humor is evident in the titles of the stone books. Her ceramic bamboo sculptures, which she named *Bambusa ceramicus* 'Chan-ticleerensis', emerge below the Chanticleer Terraces.

We don't plan to add more sculpture, other than pieces of furniture and other functional items made by our staff. As Joe Henderson puts it, "Sculpture in a garden is a tough sell. At what point does a garden become a sculpture park? There is always the temptation to make artwork a focal point. At Chanticleer, we nestle our sculp-tural pieces into the landscape so they reflect the garden and become of the garden. When I made a wrought-iron handrail for the Teacup Garden, I included dogwood flowers as a sign of respect for the magnificent dogwood adjacent to the rail. If you look closely, you'll also see dog-wood flowers on the Teacup fountain. The railing also features a snake, which I added because I was born in the Year of the Snake."

Initiation as a Chanticleer Craftsman

DOUG CROFT

Soon after starting as a horticulturist at Chanticleer, I realized there were nongardening responsibilities to the position. While former horticulturist Lisa Crock and I were transplanting pea seedlings, she explained how she and Douglas Randolph had made the Vegetable Garden gazebo using a fallen eastern red cedar. At the wood and metal shops, I saw the welder that constructed rebar arches for the Cut Flower Garden and viewed copper sheets Joe Henderson, a former jeweler, used to build the roof of a plant list box. Lying beside the copper was a coil of lead solder he used to create glass panels for another box. Joe's training as a jeweler shows in his plant list boxes throughout the garden.

As part of the daily pre-opening routine, we cleaned the furniture under the katsura trees at the Cut Flower Garden. I asked Lisa where you could buy such rustic furniture. "Oh, it was made in the woodshop by Lisa Roper." Under the Tennis Court Arbor, I saw a glider made by Doug Randolph. The next task was creating floral arrangements for the restrooms and reception desk. We went to the Ponds to harvest irises and crossed a footbridge with an arching handrail made by Przemek Walczak. Przemek was also an arborist, and his love of trees is manifested in the handrails. The base of the rails is carved to look like the buttress roots of a tree.

We passed the Apple House where the Rosengartens stored fruit. Inside, I saw a mural of a hollowed-out tree with chipmunks storing acorns, a view of Chanticleer from the underworld created by gardener Laurel Voran. She also built the wooden shelf fungus plant list box for Minder Woods. Laurel called her mural *The (Chip)munks' Hood*, and planted monkshood (*Aconitum*) nearby. Not many people catch the pun. Back at the Entrance, I set my harvesting bucket down on a bench, and a voice came up from behind: "I am going to have to ask you not to put the bucket on that bench." It was Dan Benarcik, who had made the bench.

We completed the floral arrangements and returned to the Vegetable Garden, where peas still lay on the ground. They needed a trellis and, obviously, it needed to be special. We found bamboo canes in the Potting Shed and twine. Inspired by Stonehenge, we made tall rectangular towers of the bamboo canes, each of a different height, crisscrossing twine for the peas to climb on. We had done it, a collaboration. I now knew how things get done at Chanticleer, how artistry is incorporated into the garden so each element a guest encounters is unique, meaningful, and an experience.

Joe Henderson's jewelry-making background is revealed in the intricate details of the plant list boxes, like the hand clasping a latch in Asian Woods.

The Apple House was once used by the Rosengartens to store fruit.

FROM MANY, ONE

With seven designer-gardeners, it could be a challenge to tie all the designs together as one garden. For Chanticleer to be successful visually, each area has to be of the same high quality. Although there is a competitive spirit among the gardeners, there is also great respect and friendship. They share meals together, as well as jokes, hopes, and dreams. They travel together to nearby nurseries and container warehouses as well as to other countries. They share the goal of making

Chanticleer one of the finest gardens in the world and they help each other in accomplishing their goal.

The personality and design philosophy of each gardener make the areas unique. Each gardener understands and respects the idea of a single cohesive Chanticleer experience, not seven different voices. They look both inward and outward to see that their areas relate and fuse together within the larger picture.

The Chanticleer Terraces' flowery lawn pulsates with the bright colors of *Dahlia coccinea*, *Emilia coccinea*, *Foeniculum vulgare* 'Purpureum', and *Verbena bonariensis*. The swimming pool teahouse rises in the background.

Naturalistic artistry at the Gravel Garden, ringed by *Juniperus virginiana* 'Emerald Sentinel'. *Porteranthus trifoliatus* and *Dianthus* 'Mountain Mist' rise above carpets of *Thymus praecox* subsp. *arcticus*.

PLANTS

Plants make Chanticleer the garden it is, and it's easy to see we are crazed about plants.

More than 5,000 taxa or different plants are currently accessioned and grown in the garden. These plants serve our educational mission. We joke we haven't met a plant we didn't like and, with the exception of invasive exotics, it is probably true. We order from over seventy nurseries each year, and we are given plants, cuttings, and seeds from friends, gardens, and plant societies around the globe.

We support local nurseries, garden centers, and public garden plant sales, utilize mail order specialty nurseries, and search for sources on the Internet. We buy large quantities of less expensive bare-root plants and plug trays from wholesale nurseries. We occasionally import plants and seeds from overseas, following the legal regulations. Trade shows such as the Mid-Atlantic Nursery Trade Show and the Tropical Plant Industry Expo offer new sources and tips about incipient trends.

We have limited greenhouse and cold frame space, so we focus on propagating hard-to-find plants. We grow most of our vegetables from seed. Some plants propagate themselves through runners, suckers, and self-sowing seeds. We divide some perennials, especially the expensive and rare ones. In acquiring plants for Asian Woods, most were available only in small quantities, so we divided aggressively as they grew.

Emma Seniuk expresses her excitement about new plants: "We all order from a wide variety of nurseries, sometimes ordering particular things from overseas. April is the month when the plants come piling in. We gardeners do a great dance of unpacking, organizing, and wildly planting. I also pillage plants like *Begonia grandis* and *Thalictrum rochebrunianum* from other gardeners' sections (with permission, of course). These spreading and self-sowing plants are there for the taking, and I usually leave the scene of the crime with a bag full of goodies."

PLANTS WITH PURPOSE

At Chanticleer, we look at plants as functional objects. Plants, rather than structures, hold the garden together and render the visual excitement for which it is known. No matter how much we like a plant, it doesn't go in the garden unless it has a purpose. Some examples of plant uses are:

Contributing structure and defining spaces
Screening
Color of foliage, twigs, and bark
Floral display
Texture
Softening of structures
Places for the eye to rest

We make the most of the plants we choose to put in, using some in masses, others as individual specimens, and many to meet challenges. For instance, plant information specialist Eric Hsu notes, *Salvia nemorosa* 'Caradonna' admirably flowers between the last of the spring bulbs and the beginning of early summer perennials. Given full sun, it needs no staking and reflushes again in late summer. Western red cedar (*Thuja plicata*) grows rapidly, adapts to different soils, and forms good hedging. Outside our deer fence, it thrives uneaten. We also have some

PREVIOUS PAGE The floral coils of corkscrew vine (*Vigna caracalla*) mimic snails.

challenging plants, which we willingly cosset while young and place in specific sites. *Draba ramosissima*, a restricted endemic of limestone cliffs in the Appalachian Mountains, prospers only in the sunny gravel beds on the margins of Bell's Run. *Epilobium canum*, a West Coast native fuschia rarely seen here, returns reliably each year in a sloping Gravel Garden bed that mimics its chaparral habitat in California.

We are unsentimental about removing plants. When their function is past, so are they. This process rejuvenates spaces and fuels ideas for plants that will work better in the design or theme of an area. We removed two 'Blue Ice' cypresses after their size became disproportionate with the gateway to the swimming pool. The freed spaces led to a revamped planting that introduced foxtail lilies (*Eremurus himalaicus*), sea kale (*Crambe maritima*), and *Allium* 'White Giant', creating a more open and floriferous display.

LEFT A hummingbird attractant with red tubular flowers, the California native fuschia (*Epilobium canum*) has readily spread through underground rhizomes in the Gravel Garden.

RIGHT The straight lines of the Chanticleer Terraces are softened with naturalistic plantings. Tulips are geometrically organized in the boxwood-edged beds to offer formality, but bring playfulness when loosely scattered in the nearby flowery lawn. Using the same yellow color ties the formal and informal together.

Echinacea tennesseensis has a look of wildness missing from some overbred *Echinacea* cultivars. This endangered species, restricted to cedar glades in central Tennessee, resents heavy clay soils but enjoys the Gravel Garden's free-draining dry soil.

Choosing Plants for the Garden

EMMA SENIUK

Each plant has its own character and personality; each part is important. How long does it flower? What is its height? Are the leaves strong enough visually to stand on their own? Does the flower face upward, looking at you like a friendly face, or does it hang down, bashful, as if hiding a secret? How are the leaves held? What is the branching structure? Can you "see through" the plant? The emerging foliage of *Aquilegia chrysantha* 'Denver Gold', for example, makes a lovely rosette of frilly foliage, concealing the soil below. In contrast, the emerging foliage of *Aquilegia* 'McKana's Giants' is fanned out and thin; the eye looks through the crown to the soil beneath.

A gardener must have a critical eye for the relative contributions of plants in the garden. Even when a garden display is beautiful, we analyze how it can be improved. Would a yellow flower lend itself to the mix? Should I augment this tulip planting next year? In a quizzical manner, we ask, how can this design be improved?

The personality of a plant also affects the style of the area where it is planted. Is the plant best as a lone specimen in a pot or is it better used repetitively throughout a bed like a self-sown wildflower? What can we add to make the planting sing? Gardening in the Cut Flower and Vegetable Gardens, I use plants to fit the parameters of my sections and then I push the envelope. Any plant with foliage or flowers usable for cutting fresh or dried is fodder for the Cut Flower area, and likewise, any edibles are welcome in the Vegetable Garden. I also listen to the desires of the staff. When I have requests for leeks, more leeks are incorporated. With cut flowers, I plant for a succession of bloom to please both the visitor and the flower arranger.

To produce enough flowers for the arrangements each week and still have a vibrant display, I lean on annuals. Annuals put out a profusion of color and bloom, and then their space can be cleared for another plant to carry on through the remainder of the season. Most annuals grow easily from seeds or cuttings and are great tools for combinations in the garden. What would a tulip be without a few companions by its side, such as forget-me-nots or wheat seedlings? A missed opportunity surely. Annuals create instant excitement. They bump up against bulbs, perennials, and other annuals in the garden with a smile, and say, "Come here often?" Certainly there could be nothing that provides as much drama in the garden and as much fun for the gardener as fresh annuals.

One of my favorite annuals for the Cut Flower Garden is *Verbena bonariensis*. It is an unusual annual with wiry but strong branching, topped off by little purple gibletlike flowers that flow rhythmically through the garden. Strawflower (*Xerochrysum bracteatum*) has out-of-this-world flowers with papery bracts as glossy as the hood of a garage-kept Corvette. They open to reveal a bright yellow center and may be cut and dried, with vibrant color that remains for over a year.

The backbone of the Cut Flower Garden is mostly late-season perennials, and I layer in bulbs, annuals, biennials, climbers, and tender plants like dahlias for a late-season crescendo. Good perennials are a must, and when I find a good perennial, I say increase it! *Rudbeckia* 'Herbstsonne' has a strong upright form, bright green foliage, daisylike yellow flowers, and it blooms valiantly through the heat of summer when not much else can stand the weather. Come autumn, I divide it and move it around the garden. I can't resist building on success.

Experimenting with New Plants

LISA ROPER

We are not afraid to try new things, and throwing caution to the wind is an excellent way to learn. Whether it's a new plant, combination, or growing technique, we experiment in public view.

Some plant marriages are not successful. For instance, I was not happy with my pairing of *Primula sieboldii* and *Epimedium rhizomatosum* in Asian Woods. Both tolerate dry shade, so I thought they might combine beautifully. The primrose is vigorous, with puckered, rounded leaves, blooming in mid-spring in colors ranging from white to fuchsia pink. It survives summer drought by going dormant. The epimedium produces spidery yellow flowers and heart-shaped leaves that are reddish when they emerge. Turns out, even though the epimedium is a rhizomatous spreader, it is not vigorous, and the primrose shaded it out in the spring.

Later, I discovered that *Epimedium perralderianum*, a vigorous spreader with the added feature of evergreen foliage, grows well with the primrose. Late emergers, such as toad lily (*Tricyrtis*) or *Begonia grandis*, also combine well with the primrose because they start growing as it is going dormant.

Plants Defining Spaces

Plants and planting beds define our garden spaces, create open and closed areas, and frame views. Long grass creates rivers of space under the Orchard's crabapples and accentuates the linear effect of Bell's Run. In the Bulb Meadow and the Ruin Meadow, we mow the paths and edges, effectively creating several large beds of long grass. The cut edges show we haven't neglected the area, distinguishing these areas from abandoned fields.

Large and small trees are especially good for defining spaces. Japanese cedars informally partition Asian Woods from the Pond Garden. Yellow magnolias announce the transition between the Orchard and the Ruin Garden. Tuliptrees and beeches, remnants of a once larger forest, loosely trace Bell's Run. The view down the hill from the Chanticleer House is bordered by trees, making the focus more controlled than if it were a wide open field. When you are sitting in a rocking chair at the top of the hill, your view is framed by the branches of a towering silver linden (*Tilia tomentosa*). Although the tree looks old, we acquired it as a small tree in 1985. In a similar manner, two katsuras (*Cercidiphyllum japonicum*) anchor and frame the long vista of the Cut Flower Garden. Intentional or not, both sexes of this dioecious species were planted together and have different silhouettes. In autumn, their cotton-candylike scent is perceptible.

Take away all of these trees and the mystery and romance of Chanticleer would be gone, as well as the anticipation of each different area. The property would be an open, rolling field. The Rosengartens, with prescience, planted their estate with trees that now bless Chanticleer with maturity and structure. The original farmland they purchased

TOP   Directing foot traffic, the mown greensward sculpts through the long grass in the Orchard, swooping around a paperbark maple (*Acer griseum*).

Silver linden (*Tilia tomentosa*) narrows the viewer's perspective from the Overlook to the Serpentine and Pond Garden. Without the tree, the eye would wander restlessly over the view.

A handsome hybrid oak, *Quercus ×saulii*, flanks the west side of Emily's House.

This young white oak (*Quercus alba*) by the Long Border may stand in the shadow of the larger tree, but its moment of mature glory will undoubtedly arrive.

OPPOSITE   What appears to be a grove of young American sycamores (*Platanus occidentalis*) by the Pond Arbor is actually stump sprouts from a lightning-struck tree.

The varying triangular shapes of *Juniperus virginiana* 'Emerald Sentinel', *Metasequoia glyptostroboides,* and *Picea abies* hold together this grouping of various conifers.

can't plant a small tree directly under a large tree because the older tree will shade the younger one and its roots will out-compete it. Instead of planting a literal replacement, we planted two future specimens nearby. These young pin oaks are distinctly pyramidal with drooping lower branches but will become widespreading in maturity. Pin oaks grow as well on the hilltop as they do in the low, damp area below the Serpentine next to a swamp white oak. Acid soil prevents pin oak from having yellow leaves from iron chlorosis, a problem in alkaline soils.

Uphill from this grouping is a red maple (*Acer rubrum*). It, too, tolerates both dry and wet soils and rewards us with scarlet fall color. A nearby grouping of young lindens was planted in 2010 and they will be as large as the maple in a decade or two. Other majestic native trees on the property include hickories, beeches, nyssas, tuliptrees, sugar maples, and black walnuts. Black walnut (*Juglans nigra*) becomes an impressive specimen, with arching branches reaching far from the trunk. The Bulb Meadow has two black walnuts; the curved branches of one frames the view toward the Rock Ledge and the stone furniture of the Gravel Garden. This nut tree is stunningly magnificent but also a nuisance. Its nuts can trip people, drop on heads, and weigh down branches. The nuts are delicious, but encased in such hard coats that most go uneaten. Seedlings come up everywhere and their vigorous taproots resist removal.

Sorrel tree (*Oxydendrum arboreum*) is not as tall as the red maple and black walnut trees, reaching up to about 40 feet. It blooms with lily-of-the-valleylike white flowers in midsummer and has spectacular red autumn color. It is not an easy tree to grow, requiring acidic, moist, organically rich but well-drained soils, a combination most gardens don't have. Minder Woods seems to have just what the species needs, and we have several big specimens. It blooms and has the best fall color in full sun, but will also tolerate shade.

White and green ash (*Fraxinus americana* and *F. pennsylvanica*) are attractive native trees, but the emerald ash borer is decimating the genus from the Midwest eastward and has been found nearby. We are watching our ash trees and applying prophylactic treatment to the largest specimen, which stands by the Pond Arbor. This pest is yet another reminder to plant a diversity of trees. With our wide range of tree species, we will not be wiped out by this insect, just very sad.

We used to have several large European beeches (*Fagus sylvatica*), both copper-leaved and cut-leaf selections. Unfortunately, European beeches seem to have a limited lifespan in this region. We lost a majestic seventy-five-year-old fernleaf beech near the Orchard when it succumbed to *Phytophthora* root rot. Fortunately, several branches of the specimen had rooted into the soil and those youngsters remain as reminders of the great tree.

Red maple (*Acer rubrum*) is ablaze in its autumn foliage, calling attention to the russet tones of the sorghum in the Serpentine.

Evening light highlights the distinctive broad pyramidal form of silver linden (*Tilia tomentosa*) by the Chanticleer House.

LEFT   Our black walnut (*Juglans nigra*) trees seen throughout the garden were once planted as financial safeguards when the area was largely agricultural because their high-quality wood fetches high prices.

Tree Maintenance

Big trees are not quickly replaced and are an investment to be treasured. We avoid cutting roots and compacting the soil around trees, two frequent killers of large trees. Grounds manager Peter Brindle and horticulturist Przemek Walczak inspect our trees in winter and in summer. Many specimens are cabled to provide support, and eighteen have lightning protection.

Horticulturist Doug Croft trains young trees to have strong branching structure in order to prevent major and expensive problems as they age. The strongest tree will have a single leader, or trunk, and branches with wide angles coming off the trunk. He inspects young trees every winter, when leaves don't hide the structure. If a tree has two or more leaders (codominants),

he selects the strongest leader and reduces the size of the others. Small competing leaders can be eliminated immediately; larger ones should be reduced over several years. Extra care is needed with evergreens, since foliage hides the structure.

We also remove dead, diseased, and dying branches. We scout for rubbing or crossing branches. We decide which to eliminate by reviewing the health of the branches and deciding which will be best in the long run for the tree. We encourage branches with wide branch angles and diameters less than 50 percent of the main trunk's diameter. We bring in professional arborists where climbing is required and to advise on pruning.

Planting Under Mature Trees

As trees mature, maintaining turf beneath them becomes more difficult. Research shows turf is a strong competitor with trees and both perform better away from each other. We have replaced lawns under trees with fern glades, beds of sedges and mosses, and, under the hybrid oak west of the house at the Entrance, mixed perennial beds. Such plantings discourage foot traffic on the tree's root zone and eliminate weekly mowing, a significant source of harmful compaction. We now have attractive beds protecting the root systems of the trees. We do not irrigate under the trees, unless the trees themselves need the water. Dan Benarcik and Jonathan Wright have used an AIR-SPADE to remove turf without herbicides or digging that might harm the trees. This tool blasts away soil without cutting tree roots, a service provided by some arborists. Following the spading, Dan and Jonathan added aged leaf compost and gently raked it to grade the new bed.

The fern beds we have established under trees consist of native *Dryopteris erythrosora* 'Brilliance' (noted for its reddish fronds), *Polystichum acrostichoides* (called Christmas fern because of its evergreen nature), and *Dryopteris ×australis* (a naturally occurring hybrid called Dixie wood fern).

Under the hybrid oak, we chose a bed of low perennials to match the surrounding plantings. Jonathan planted plugs of *Anemone sylvestris* and *Phlox stolonifera* 'Sherwood Purple' in ribbons along the meandering, large roots to enhance a feeling of movement. Small patches of

Replacing the turf underneath this venerable hybrid oak (*Quercus* ×*saulii*) with mixed perennial plantings eliminates mowing, protects the tree's root zone, and boosts visual appeal.

Epimedium ×youngianum 'Niveum' and *Carex eburnea* soften the composition. To bridge the plantings and tie the new bed into the existing garden, he lifted and divided nearby *Hosta* 'Golden Tiara', *Heuchera* 'Montrose Ruby', and *Hakonechloa macra* 'Aureola' and accented with scilla, chionodoxa, and multiflowering *Hyacinthus orientalis* 'Blue Festival'. The divisions and purchased plugs were all small, allowing planting gently with fingers, further protecting the tree's roots.

Planting Trees for the Future

We plant trees for the canopy of the future, selecting appropriate species for each location. We try to choose a young tree with a single, dominant leader and a healthy root system, and avoid trees that are root-bound or planted too deeply. Starting with small, young trees that transplant readily allows us to train both the roots and the top of the plant. We gently check the root collar of each new tree (the point where the roots come out from the trunk), which should be slightly above the ground when planted. Bare-root trees are ideal for checking roots, but require extra care to ensure the roots do not dry out before you get the tree in the ground.

There is an epidemic of poorly grown trees in nurseries. Many have spiraling roots from being in containers too long and many are planted too deeply. Trees planted too deeply do not thrive and are much more likely to have circling (strangling) roots. We have found balled-and-burlapped trees planted as much as 10 inches too deep. Spiraling roots never straighten out and eventually kill the tree, wasting many years of growth. We sometimes bare-root a containerized tree and straighten the roots to get a good root system. We did this with some pots of 6-foot-tall *Chamaecyparis obtusa* we were given. The roots tightly circled the pot and we knew the plants would not live long that way. But the species is very difficult to find, so we spent over an hour on each plant, washing the soil off the roots and then straightening them in the planting hole. We made sure the trees never dried out, but they were yellowish for the first two years and grew very little. By the third year, the foliage was green and the plants began to grow.

Replacement of trees in a symmetrical setting is a challenge. For example, the flowering cherries around the Gravel Circle at the Chanticleer House form a unit. If one dies, it leaves a hole. You could replace all the trees at once so they are the same size, but that requires cutting down healthy trees. Instead, we replace trees as they die. If you look closely at the circle, you'll notice the trees are not all the same age and size. The fast growth rate of flowering cherry trees helps overcome the age difference.

The Usefulness of Willows

Willows are often disregarded in the tree world. Their wood is soft and the fast-growing trees do not live to be old specimens. However, willows are very useful. Because of their rapid growth, they fill in areas quickly. Most species root easily, and branches stuck directly in the soil become small trees within a couple of years. They resprout from hard pruning, so a damaged tree can be cut to the ground and, within a year, new sprouts will grow from the stump, which can then be thinned to a single trunk or it can be allowed to become a bushy plant.

Some willows, such as *Salix chaenomeloides* and *S. caprea*, have showy flowers in late winter. The branches of these pussy willows will root in water for later planting outside. When the shrub gets too big, simply cut it to the ground and let it regrow. At the entrance to the Ruin, you'll see *Salix caprea* 'Pendula', with weeping branches, and *S. caprea* 'Ogon', which has yellow leaves. Other willows with colorful leaves (brightest with new growth) are *Salix sachalinensis* 'Golden Sunshine' with yellow leaves and *S. integra* 'Alba Maculata' with bright white, pink-tipped leaves in spring.

Salix alba 'Britzensis' has red winter twigs, which turn green in the summer, and narrow silvery leaves. The leaves resemble those of olive trees, so we've used them as "mock olives" in the Teacup Garden and the Serpentine. The Serpentine trees were started by directly sticking 3-foot-long cuttings in the ground. To give the feeling of age, we stuck three stems in the ground and wove them together. 'Britzensis' branches give colorful height to our spring containers. Rosemary willow (*S. elaeagnos*) has gray leaves that also resemble olive leaves. In the Teacup Garden, we've espaliered them up walls, pruned them like poodles, and let some grow naturally (10 feet high by 10 feet wide). Nearby, *S.* 'Golden Curls' seems vinelike because of its twisted, corkscrewlike, weeping, yellow branches. We use the cut branches decoratively in spring containers and to stake plants, and the rooted branches give us new plants. In Bell's Woodland, Przemek Walczak lined paths with hoops of cut willows. The hoops have become living fences and each year he prunes and weaves them together.

The fat, silvery catkins of giant pussy willow (*Salix chaenomeloides*) in the Ruin Garden bristle with yellow-orange anthers.

Rooted cuttings of *Salix sachalinensis* 'Golden Sunshine' are loosely cordoned among overlapping hoops, hiding the public restrooms from sight. The willow's chartreuse foliage remains vivid throughout the growing season.

The orange stems of *Salix alba* 'Britzensis' in the Serpentine seemingly glow brighter under a dusting of snow. Multiple young stems emerged last season at the cut ends.

The ease with which cut willow stems root when stuck in the ground encouraged Bell's Woodland horticulturist Przemek Walczak to use them as fencing. Because the willows grow rapidly, they need regular pruning and weaving to maintain the fences' distinctiveness.

Stuck as vertical accents in containers, the orange stems of *Salix alba* 'Britzensis' are cut in the spring and contrast startlingly with purple wallflowers (*Erysimum* 'Winter Joy' and *E.* 'Winter Orchid').

We have even woven hanging baskets with colorful willow stems, making the baskets attractive and colorful. Dogwood (*Cornus sericea*) stems work equally well. Some of the Japanese maples (*Acer palmatum*) also have colorful twigs, but they don't tolerate hard pruning the way willows and dogwoods do. In the Ruin Meadow, *A. palmatum* 'Sango kaku' has red winter twigs. The orange winter twigs of *Acer palmatum* 'Bi hoo' harmonize compellingly with those of *Cornus sanguinea* 'Arctic Sun' in the Teacup Garden and Tennis Court.

Conifers

Evergreens form a dark background for the bright blossoms of spring flowering trees and provide vivid contrast to autumn colors. In summer, evergreens almost disappear as they merge into the background, but they rule the winter landscape, and nothing beats them for screening any time of the year. Evergreen plants remain fully leaved throughout the year. The leaves drop but never all at once. Pines, for instance, drop their older needles in autumn, but retain at least one year's worth of leaves.

In winter, evergreens become the stars of screening and defining space as deciduous trees drop their leaves. Narrow, shade-tolerant evergreens are best for screening. The narrow width is more easily staggered and grouped, while shade tolerance allows the tree to retain the lower branches. Shade-intolerant pines are not useful for screening because

OPPOSITE *Picea orientalis* delineates the boundary between the Ruin Meadow and the Creek Garden.

The columnar spires of Japanese cedar (*Cryptomeria japonica* 'Yoshino') in Asian Woods provide a dark green backdrop for the awakening spring splendor of the Pond Garden.

Framed by the Ruin's window, *Picea abies* 'Pendula' resembles snow-clad, lumbering creatures in a wintry landscape.

they are widespreading and lose their lower branches. To achieve a more naturalistic evergreen screen, we avoid straight lines, mix up the spacing, and vary the size of the individual trees. A screening of evergreens creates a microclimate the same way a wall does. A solid planting of evergreens south of the Apple House keeps the walkway icy and delays the bloom of *Crocus tommasinianus*. Conversely, the evergreens of the Creek Garden and the Winter Shrub Border block the wind and make those areas warmer.

Excellent evergreen trees for screening are cedars (*Thuja plicata*, *T.* 'Green Giant', *Cryptomeria japonica* 'Yoshino') and spruces (*Picea orientalis*, *P. abies)*. Plant snobs often look down upon thujas, considering arborvitaes common plants. We've found *Thuja* 'Green Giant' and *T. plicata* to be elegant, single-stemmed, fast-growing plants. They are superior to the more common *T. occidentalis*, which is browsed by deer, susceptible to bagworms, and often multistemmed (thus susceptible to splaying, or bending outward, in winter storms). With strong central leaders, *T. plicata* and *T.* 'Green Giant' are rarely bothered by snow and ice. Growing at least 3 feet per year, they quickly screen and tolerate sun or shade. They need moderate soil drainage, but can tolerate some wetness to the soil.

Japanese cedar (*Cryptomeria japonica* 'Yoshino') grows equally fast and is tolerant of sun or shade, but less tolerant of dry soils in the sun (where they are susceptible to mites). This cultivar doesn't brown in the winter like the species. Thujas and cryptomerias resprout on old wood when pruned hard, as long as light is able to reach the cut area. All are narrow enough to be useful in most garden settings. *Thuja* 'Green Giant' is the narrowest, only about 6 feet wide. *Thuja plicata* is a bit wider and *Cryptomeria japonica* 'Yoshino' reaches about 15 feet wide. Ultimate height for all three is about 80 feet.

Spruces are shaped like traditional Christmas trees. *Picea orientalis* is native to the Balkans (not Asia) and is our healthiest and prettiest spruce. Its dark foliage sets a somber mood near the creek and by the Apple House. We've used it along roadways to screen out surrounding properties, roads, and utilities and to provide a backdrop to flowering plants. *Picea orientalis* has a narrow pyramidal form reaching 60 feet high and 20 feet wide. Its northern European relative, *P. abies*, is big in width (40 feet) and height (100 feet) and grows quickly in almost any condition. A tall one shades the Orchard walkway and was the Rosengarten's living Christmas tree in 1917.

Deciduous Conifers for Texture

Deciduous conifers offer a combination of fine texture, height, and autumn color. Four dawn redwoods (*Metasequoia glyptostroboides*), planted in 1993, quickly filled the Entrance. Their growth has slowed, perhaps because of a hardpan of construction soil beneath them and the limits of the surrounding pavement. Our largest metasequoia grows

near the Serpentine, where it grows strongly with a distinctive point to its top. We think Adolph Jr. planted it in the 1970s. Metasequoias are the last deciduous trees to turn color in autumn, waiting until late autumn to drop their then rusty orange leaves. As the leaves drop, we know winter is near.

Bald cypress (*Taxodium distichum*) is similar, with alternately arranged leaves versus metasequoia's opposite leaves. Bald cypress "knees" grow from the roots to a height of about 2 feet and look a bit like human knees. Cypress knees are abundant in the upper Creek Garden. Pond cypress, *Taxodium distichum* var. *imbricatum*, is a narrow tree and stands gracefully by the Ruin. Its threadlike leaves have the finest texture of the conifers and a bluish green color; they emerge upright in the spring as if startled. In winter, the fine twigs set off the distinctly horizontal branches. Autumn color on both taxodiums is rusty orange.

Larches look so much like evergreens they surprise nongardeners when they drop their needles in the fall. The needles are whorled on short spur shoots. *Larix decidua*, European larch, is a fast grower; several young specimens are quickly becoming trees in the Winter Shrub Border. Nearby stand several golden larches (*Pseudolarix amabilis*) with longer needles and spur shoots. They are more challenging to grow, requiring excellent drainage yet ample moisture, and ours grow slowly. An older one is across the lawn above the Serpentine.

LEFT *Metasequoia glyptostroboides* 'Gold Rush', towering over the Pond Garden Spring House, trades its chartreuse summer needles for autumnal auburn.

RIGHT Not a true larch (*Larix*) but the sole representative of its genus related to pines, false larch (*Pseudolarix amabilis*) turns a radiant golden yellow in autumn. Pseudolarix grows well in areas of summer heat and humidity where true larches might fail.

Pines, Firs, and Hemlocks for Bold Textural Effects

Pines are our largest evergreen trees and make picturesque specimens. The loose habit of the native eastern white pine (*Pinus strobus*) shades the teahouse by the Chanticleer Pool and the Ruin. It has five needles to a bundle, like all the species of white pines. It is easy to love the trees' rustic, informal feel, at least until an ice storm causes them to lose branches. Less likely to drop branches are *Pinus strobus* 'Fastigiata' (a cultivar that is narrow as a young tree, becoming two-thirds the width of the species at maturity), *P. wallichiana* (Himalayan white pine, similar to *P. strobus* but with longer, drooping needles), and *P. koraiensis* (Korean white pine, with long, thick needles remaining on the tree several years longer than the previous two species, giving it a fuller appearance).

Two more five-needled pines make statements in the garden. The narrow *Pinus cembra* grows along the walkway between the upper and lower parking lots. An impressive, picturesque *P. parviflora* 'Glauca' stands near the Serpentine. The needles have a bluish cast that contrasts beautifully for a week in the spring with the expanding pink male cone buds. Several young trees of the species are planted in the basins next to the Serpentine. They are seedlings of seeds collected in the wild in South Korea by the Morris and U.S. National Arboretums.

Several loblolly pines (*Pinus taeda*), with three needles to the bundle, border the bus parking lot. Normally beautiful trees, our plants have yellowish needles and are not vigorous. Soil issues may be at play, as could a lack of hardiness. Two-needled pines are often hit by fungus in our climate. A large specimen of the two-needled *P. sylvestris* (Scots pine) stands in Minder Woods, but is so closely surrounded by other pines that only its reddish orange bark stands out. A *P. nigra* (Austrian pine) grows next to it, another tree with fungal issues in our region, yet this one survives. Find it by searching for its whitish bark. On the Rock Ledge above the Ponds, two dwarf cultivars of *P. thunbergii* ('Thunderhead' and 'Kyokko') live. Although slow-growing, we prune them to keep them lower and tighter, breaking the candles (the new growth) before the needles have expanded. New buds form wherever the candle is broken, an effective technique with any pine.

Most species of firs (genus *Abies*) have difficulty with summer heat. An exception is *A. nordmanniana*; a grouping reigns in the upper portion of the Orchard near the Ruin. Other healthy firs for this area include *A. holophylla* (near the Asian Woods Restrooms), *A. firma* (Parking Lot), and *A. concolor* (Minder Woods). Often mistaken for blue Colorado spruce, white fir (*A. concolor*) has soft (not prickly) bluish needles. An *A. koreana* 'Silberlocke' specimen holds court at the base of the Tennis Court steps. This dwarf is distinctly silver because the needles are sharply curved, exposing their glaucous undersides. Blues, purples, and pinks of clematis look stunning scrambling over the silvery foliage.

A grove of eastern white pine (*Pinus strobus*) fans out behind the swimming pool teahouse.

Canada hemlock (*Tsuga canadensis*) is the state tree of Pennsylvania. We once had a number of specimens, including a hedge around the Chanticleer Terraces. Since the 1970s, however, the tree has been severely attacked by several pests, including woolly adelgid. We replaced the hedge with *Thuja plicata* 'Atrovirens' and now spray our remaining hemlocks with horticultural oil, an organic practice, to keep them healthy. Luckily, *Tsuga canadensis* 'Pendula' is less susceptible to the pests. We have two large specimens of this spreading conifer below the Gravel and Tennis Court Gardens. The Morris Arboretum has collected seeds in China of *T. chinensis*, the only hemlock species that thrives in our hot summers and is pest-resistant. We have trees of this species at the Parking Lot Garden and scattered throughout Chanticleer.

Small Evergreen Trees for Screens

Height is not always needed in plants you want to use as screens. American holly (*Ilex opaca*) is a tough, small, evergreen tree. Female plants produce showy red berries but need males for pollination. *Ilex opaca* and cultivars grow in Bell's Woodland and throughout the property. A holly massing at the base of the Orchard screens it from the Creek Garden, creating garden rooms. 'Miss Helen' and 'Old Heavy Berry' are among the best female cultivars. We have a few plants of *I. opaca* 'Satyr Hill', the 2003 American Holly Society Holly of the Year. It was found as a volunteer female seedling at McLean Nurseries in Towson, Maryland, named for the road on which the nursery is located. It has wide, flattish, slightly glossy leaves. The berries often stay on the plant until late winter, when they are eaten by birds.

American hollies have dull leaves. For luster, we use 'Dragon Lady', 'James G. Esson', 'Doctor Kassab', 'Nellie R. Stevens', and Foster hollies (*Ilex ×attenuata* 'Foster #2'). *Ilex pedunculosa*, found in Minder Woods, has leaves that lack spiny points, causing many to think it is not a holly. Nearby in Minder Woods, healthy floriferous *Pieris japonica* plants thrive in the rich, moist soil and year-round shade. When grown in full sun, they tend to be pest-ridden. Its showy American cousin, *P. floribunda*, is nearly impossible to find in the trade and has yet to thrive for us. Sigh.

Southern magnolia (*Magnolia grandiflora*) is both evergreen and the best loved magnolia. Valued for its huge blossoms that are especially fragrant at night, it is perfect placed near patios where people gather in the early evening. The species is borderline hardy here, but 'Edith Bogue' and the smaller 'Bracken's Brown Beauty' have been the hardiest for us. We've espaliered 'Little Gem' against the wall near the reflecting pool on the Chanticleer Terrace, but it can suffer in some of our winters.

Magnolia virginiana varies from being totally deciduous to being evergreen. 'Green Shadow' (formerly 'Green Bay') is reliably evergreen,

CLOCKWISE FROM TOP LEFT White fir (*Abies concolor*) is a heat-tolerant fir with soft blue needles.

A trio of Canada hemlock (*Tsuga canadensis*), with the characteristic nodding hemlock tops, conceals deer fencing near Bell's Run.

Given its wandering span of weeping branches and textural variations, a large specimen of *Tsuga canadensis* 'Pendula' looks animated above the Pond Arbor.

TOP LEFT   Growing near the edge of Minder Woods, longstalk holly (*Ilex pedunculosa*) sports attractive red berries held on long stalks (pedicles), giving the effect of dangling earrings.

TOP RIGHT   *Magnolia virginiana*, an evergreen to semideciduous native species, emits a lovely lemon fragrance on balmy summer days.

BOTTOM   More narrow than the species itself, 'Green Arrow' Alaska cedar (*Xanthocyparis nootkatensis* 'Green Arrow') is a distinctive conifer that ties together the Long Border.

OPPOSITE   Two *Chamaecyparis obtusa* 'Fastigiata' cypress mark the base of the Ruin Meadow next to the drinking fountain.

'Henry Hicks' is almost as reliable, and 'Moonglow' (formerly 'Jim Wilson') is only somewhat evergreen. The original 'Henry Hicks' at the Scott Arboretum is fully evergreen. Grafted offspring are partially deciduous for us and shed leaves throughout the year. Plant information specialist Eric Hsu thinks the grafted rootstock influences the scion. Both of these magnolia species and American hollies tolerate wet as well as dry soils.

The cypress genus *Chamaecyparis* is known better for its cultivars than for the species themselves. *Chamaecyparis obtusa* has dark green, scaly foliage and does beautifully in our climate in sun and shade. The straight species is difficult to find, but makes a beautiful tree 70 feet tall and 25 feet wide. Slower growing *C. obtusa* 'Gracilis' and 'Nana Gracilis' are smaller than the species. 'Aurea Nana' is a tight dwarf with yellow-tinged foliage. A curving line of the closely related Alaska yellow cedar (*Xanthocyparis* [formerly *Chamaecyparis*] *nootkatensis* 'Green Arrow') runs like a spine through the Long Border. These plants are tall, bluish green in color, and narrow because of drooping side branches. They cast little shade on this perennial border but have arresting visual qualities that mark this area of the garden.

Color Flow in the Garden

Much of Chanticleer's color comes from foliage. Flowers are accents, like cameos in a movie—important, but not the stars. Leaves last all season, whereas flowers may only last a few weeks.

Next to the Pond Garden, *Catalpa bignonioides* 'Aurea' leads a theme of yellow, spreading its broad canopy of chartreuse leaves over similarly hued bamboo (*Pleioblastus viridistriatus*), which is echoed across the water by a golden metasequoia and a yellow-leaved willow. In the Pond Garden itself, we cut back the yellow catalpas hard each winter, resulting in larger, bolder leaves the following season. Herbaceous yellow flowers flow through the beds (thermopsis and verbascums in early summer, moving on to *Patrinia*, *Inula*, and *Silphium* in the summer, and perennial sunflowers in the autumn). Adding to the aesthetic theme, goldfinches feed on the many seed heads, adding flashes of yellow to the scene.

The Long Border has a yellow foliage theme flowing throughout the season, with floral accents coming and going. Trees hold the border together, including the yellow-leaved *Cercis canadensis* 'Hearts of Gold' and *Robinia pseudoacacia* 'Frisia', *Picea orientalis* 'Skylands', and the contrasting bluish green of *Xanthocyparis nootkatensis* 'Green Arrow'. On the ground plane, yellow leaves of *Symphytum ×uplandicum* 'Axminster Gold', *Juniperus horizontalis* 'Mother Lode', *Hosta* 'Feather Boa', and *Acorus gramineus* 'Ogon' pull the eye and combine with the yellow flowers of *Phlomis russeliana*. White clouds of *Crambe cordifolia* and *C. maritima* and the blue flowers of *Anchusa azurea* complement the yellow.

TOP   The bright yellow leaves of the ground-covering bamboo (*Pleioblastus viridistriatus*) echo those of the *Catalpa bignonioides* 'Aurea'.

BOTTOM   Yellow is a thematic color at Chanticleer, beginning with the Long Border, in year-round plantings with herbaceous accents, contrasted with the white blossoms of flowering sea kale (*Crambe cordifolia*).

In the Tennis Court, the spring theme is chartreuse: Sedums lead you down the steps, and glowing in the beds are *Cercis canadensis* 'Hearts of Gold', *Spiraea ×bumalda* 'Fire Light' and 'Magic Carpet', *S. thunbergii* 'Ogon', *Thuja occidentalis* 'Yellow Ribbon', *Carex elata* 'Bowles's Golden', *Tanacetum vulgare* 'Isla Gold', *Acer palmatum* 'Bi hoo', and *Aralia cordata* 'Sun King'. Complementing the yellows are purple-flowered alliums and spireas and pink 'New Dawn' roses climbing on the arbor. Contrasting in shape are the spikes of *Thermopsis villosa*, *Baptisia*, *Iris*, *Calamagrostis ×acutiflora* 'Karl Foerster', and even the flower stalks of *Rheum palmatum* var. *tanguticum* and *Digitalis*. Shrubs on the side enclose the space, as does the arbor at the north end.

The Tennis Court Garden is aglitter with herbaceous perennials and woody plants: Purple alliums glisten jewel-like among *Cercis canadensis* 'Hearts of Gold', *Deutzia gracilis* 'Chardonnay Pearls', *Spiraea ×bumalda* 'Magic Carpet', and *Thuja occidentalis* 'Yellow Ribbon'.

Hard to find in the trade because of propagation difficulties, this comfrey (*Symphytum ×uplandicum* 'Axminster Gold') is unsurpassed for its clean variegated foliage, blue flowers, and waterfall form. We cut down the plants after flowering to encourage fresh foliage for the rest of the season.

Three Views on Color

DOUG CROFT

I think of using color in the garden like I approach investing—diversification is key. I like the security of a few diehards for color throughout the season, and I select a few high risks that when they perform well, yield a huge payoff, but if they underperform, I sell and have other "investments" waiting in the wings.

The bright yellow foliage of this hybrid comfrey (*Symphytum ×uplandicum* 'Axminster Gold') makes a strong impact in the Long Border, providing color from spring until an autumn hard frost and is reliable for years. The comfrey's blue flowers are a bonus, but its real attribute is its colorful foliage. A diehard for flower color is plume thistle (*Cirsium rivulare* 'Atropurpureum'), a perennial with many purple flowers in the summer. The flower stems are sturdy and perform well in floral arrangements.

Giant scabious (*Cephalaria gigantea*) falls into the high risk, temperamental category. With creamy yellow flowers on 6-foot stems, it is a real beauty when the plant is contented. It seems happiest in sunny, open areas but performs poorly when crowded. Lisianthus (*Eustoma grandiflorum*) is most successful when started as a plug, allowing for minimal disturbance to the roots. It takes a while for the plants to start growing, but once established and in flower, our visitors adore them.

If other investments fail, I turn to diehards like zinnias, cosmos, and marigolds (I'm fond of *Tagetes erecta* 'Linnaeus'), which germinate quickly from seed and grow well in the summer heat. I sow the seeds into plug trays and let them grow on in our cold frames, ready to fill voids during the summer. Dahlias give us reliable color in summer and fall and have a huge range of height, hue, and flower type. Seed-grown dahlias are shorter and great for the front of the border. Larger dahlias grow from tubers and can be potted up to be ready when needed or planted directly into the beds once the threat of frost has passed. Emma Seniuk uses our cold frames for starting tender tubers such as dahlias, cannas, and gloriosa lilies. She leaves the frames closed in the spring so they warm up in the sunshine, getting an early start on the plants, which will then flower in early summer.

EMMA SENIUK

Color is one of the most subjective topics in gardening. I delight in combining colors that others might consider discordant, like orange with a sparkling magenta. Color is, after all, not just color. There are hues, tones, and saturations to consider in making up each floral or foliage combination. Often a plant will have colors that play off themselves, and in those cases, we consider the whole plant. Rather than just commenting on a pink flower, the good gardener knows to acknowledge the bright yellow center, the matte purple foliage, and the delightful reddish hue in the petioles and stems.

I am attracted to the supple but operatic petals of dahlias, the classic white rays with a mustard yellow center of *Cosmos bipinnatus* 'Purity', and the sharp chartreuse of a dill umbel. Spring bedding annual grass *Lagurus ovatus* possesses a green tone that would make a lawn caretaker envious. Its clean, graceful leaves move effortlessly in the slightest breeze and the color is heightened by a coating of tiny tomentose hairs, which beautifully catch the soft light at the beginning and end of the day. Color, like so many other great things in life, is complicated.

Hot colors energize the Tennis Court Garden and are a dramatic shift from spring pastels: from *Spiraea ×bumalda* 'Goldflame' and tulips at the ground level to *Sedum rupestre* 'Angelina' and orange violas flanking the steps.

JOE HENDERSON

I am dazzled by color and want it bright, searing, and unencumbered by fashionable trends. I was recently at the Woolrich store in the town of the same name and spied a blanket of a vibrant tangerine-peel orange. I coveted that color: a truly amazing, succulent orange. My poppies lick at the warmth of the spring sun and wave in the breeze to nearby orange globeflowers. I smile at the indigo blue Japanese irises and the warm cerise of the 'Mrs. Perry D. Slocum' lotus with its huge, blue-tinged leaves. Candelabra primroses in cherry, snow white, citrus, and watermelon grow alongside pitcher plants whose maroon and chartreuse leaves resemble rotting meat to attract their pollinators.

Lurid colors love to be used with contrasting elements. A florid hillside of poppies is only as intense as the banal colors surrounding it. Green is opposite orange on the color wheel and together they make music. Intense colors are like a rich steak that needs to be balanced by a leafy green for its succulence to be fully appreciated. Overstimulation leads to less interest because each serving will be overlooked as just more excess.

Birds Add Life to the Garden

A just-fledged great horned owlet casts a piercing glance from its perch above the Ruin.

RIGHT   A juvenile American robin, one of many youngsters we see each spring, sets out tentatively to explore its brave new world that is Chanticleer.

Like most gardens, Chanticleer is filled with birds. The diversity of habitats encourages a wide range of our flying friends. We leave old tree trunks standing to encourage woodpeckers and other wildlife. Seed heads of flowers are loved by finches and other seed-eating birds. Whenever we grow sunflowers in the Serpentine, finches claim the space and hawks claim some of the finches. Herons feast on fish in the Ponds, and annually, we have several nesting pairs of northern orioles. One year, great horned owls nested in a pine near the Ruin and raised two owlets that claimed the Ruin as their own. Perhaps because of all our visitors, we haven't found owls again so close.

Autumn Foliage Color

Autumn brings another color theme to the garden, one that reaches to the sky. Starting in early autumn when the leaves of *Nyssa sylvatica* and *Oxydendrum arboreum* turn red, through late autumn when *Metasequoia glyptostroboides* finally colors russet red, our trees are a blazing show. Mid-autumn brings the greatest show of color, with *Liriodendron tulip-ifera* (yellow), *Quercus alba* and *Q. rubra* (red), *Fagus grandifolia* (rusty yellow), *Acer rubrum* and *A. buergerianum* (red), *A. saccharum* (orange), *A. griseum* (red-orange), various flowering cherries (orange), *Cornus kousa* (orange), and *C. florida* (red). As their leaves drop, the air itself swirls with color, eventually covering the ground in brilliant yellows, reds, and oranges.

Autumn is also a time to celebrate the beauty of the natural decay process. The entire garden begins to turn tan and brown, with accents of color from flowers and fruits. Seed heads on perennials stand out and declining foliage has a magic of its own. The Pond Garden is a perfect place to see this glorious autumn transition, but any of the areas with perennials (such as the Tennis Court and Gravel Gardens) are highlights at this time of the year.

Bark Color and Texture

The exfoliating bark of the stewartia grove near the Pond Arbor amazes visitors any day of the year, while the small, white, camellialike flowers are often missed in late spring until they drop onto the path below. The bark of *Stewartia pseudocamellia* is a stunning camouflage pattern of browns and creams, exfoliating in irregular, vertical patches. Near the Asian Woods Restrooms, the rusty red bark of *S. monadelpha* is perhaps the prettiest bark in the garden. Stewartias are understory trees in their native environment, they grow best in light shade and well-drained moist soil, and they have attractive maroon to orange autumn color.

Rivaling the spectacular bark of *Stewartia monadelpha* are paperbark maple (*Acer griseum*) and crepe myrtle (*Lagerstroemia*). Paperbark maple has a bright, rust-red bark and thrives in rich soil that drains perfectly. Our single specimen in the Orchard is a beautiful loner and would be visually more impressive with company. With bark, one trunk is wonderful; a grouping, memorable. Crepe myrtles are ubiquitous in the South but less common in the Mid-Atlantic because of our cold winters. We've had good success with some of the U.S. National Arboretum hybrids, which have Native American names and reddish bark because of their *Lagerstroemia fauriei* parentage. On the Chanticleer Terraces, *L.* 'Tonto' has bright magenta flowers during the summer and its bark almost begs you to touch it. A 'Tonto' seedling came up at the nearby reflecting pool and we let it grow (removing paving stones as it grew). 'Choctaw' makes a strong pink showing near our Entrance.

Trunks of *Pinus bungeana* begin exfoliating at a young age, resembling camouflage clothing. With age and exposure to wind and sun, the bark eventually becomes ghostly white. Lacebark pine requires

Acer griseum becomes more dignified with each passing year. The bark has the smoothness of the finest alabaster, the exfoliating coils more and more numerous, and the color a rich auburn hue.

Few trees rival *Stewartia pseudocamellia* in the good looks department, because of its exfoliating patchwork bark, white blossoms, and maroon fall foliage.

LEFT Our native persimmon
(*Diospyros virginiana*) has
striking scaly bark that
evokes alligator hide.

RIGHT The camouflage
bark pattern of *Pinus
bungeana* eventually
becomes a distinguished,
spectral white.

excellent soil drainage and full sun. Training the pine from a young age to have a single leader will avoid the heartbreak of a thirty-year-old, multistemmed tree splitting in an ice storm. Sycamores (*Platanus occidentalis*) are common native trees in this area, often occurring along rivers and creeks. Their bark exfoliates year-round, but especially in the summer, giving it a reputation as a messy tree. If you can get beyond the messiness, its bark is stunningly beautiful, becoming white with age. If it were rare or hard to grow, we'd all be fighting for it.

Another native with intriguing bark is *Diospyros virginiana*. This native persimmon doesn't have colorful bark, but it has such an interesting texture it stops most guests in their tracks. It grows at the base of the Bulb Meadow, on the edge of Asian Woods, and is one of the largest of this species we have seen—tall and thin, with beautifully grooved bark. Two young trees grow across the path, which were suckers that grew from the roots of the older tree. A male, it doesn't produce fruit, but pollinates a female in the Pond Garden.

Spring Favorites: Flowering Cherries

Flowering trees are dual performers, fulfilling the needs of the garden for structure and floriferous beauty. They define spaces throughout the year and, because of their smaller scale, they may perform this function better than tall trees. Small flowering trees have the bonus of flower color, often followed by attractive fruits and fall foliage color.

Flowering cherries are spectacular spring-blooming trees. Give them ample sunlight and good drainage, and they will perform well. Most present yellow to orange autumn foliage color and have attractive bark. Their fruit, if produced, is neither showy nor tasty (even though related to the cherries we eat).

Prunus 'Accolade' encloses the Gravel Circle at the Chanticleer House, serving as a living wall. The pink, semidouble flowers of this hybrid of Sargent and Higan flowering cherries (*P. sargentii* and *P. ×subhirtella*) complement the color of the puce-toned gravel and the house's cream stucco. The raked gravel here is inspired by Japanese Zen gardens; the most beautiful moment of this spot is when the cherries bloom in early spring and drop petals onto the gravel. This fleeting

It is a sublimely pleasant moment when the petals of *Prunus* 'Accolade' drift into the grooves of the raked Gravel Circle.

Selections of flowering cherries vary in their mature forms, as evident in (left) the cloudlike *Prunus* 'Accolade' and (right) the tighter, vaselike *Prunus* 'Dream Catcher'.

performance lasts but a few days. *Prunus* 'Dream Catcher', an offspring of *P*. 'Okame', has a bloom similar to 'Accolade' with a more upright growth habit. It's planted along the walkway to the Ruin and behind the Vegetable Garden. *Prunus sargentii* is a pink-blooming species we admired at Delaware's Winterthur Garden. Several grow in the upper part of the Orchard, where they bloom near their offspring "Accolade'. The autumn foliage color is orange.

Prunus ×*yedoensis*, the famous Japanese flowering cherry of Washington, D.C., shades the picnic area near the Vegetable Garden. *Prunus* ×*subhirtella* 'Autumnalis' hovers over the reflecting pool on the Chanticleer Terraces. The concept of a cherry tree that blooms in the fall and again in the spring sounds great, but in reality, the autumn blossoms of 'Autumnalis' are weak as is the spring display. The tree also is unattractively twiggy. Joe Henderson espaliered 'Snow Fountain' cherry against the stone wall of the Pond Arbor. Its vinelike effect repeats the shape of the nearby wisterias and has fooled many a horticultural student. When we were offered a poorly shaped specimen of the same cultivar, Joe planted it on its side above the arbor, where its drooping leaves on wired branches have an effect similar to its neighbor.

Other Amazing Flowering Trees

Just as the flowering cherries finish their show in early spring, our native redbuds take center stage. *Cercis canadensis* is a multistemmed tree 20 to 30 feet tall with pealike purplish rose flowers on bare branches. An understory tree, it tolerates sun or shade and its seedlings abound in the upper part of Bell's Woodland. Not long-lived, it will often resprout if cut to the ground. *Cercis canadensis* 'Alba' has stunningly crisp, white flowers that are more easily used in a garden. More shrublike and floriferous, *C. chinensis* can become weedy. Our giant redbud (*C. gigantea*) near the Entrance Pavilion is rare and produces purple, pealike pods.

Once a working apple and cherry orchard, the Orchard is now planted with crabapples, Japanese flowering cherries, and other ornamental trees. Crabapples (*Malus* spp.) have showy flowers, small fruits, and vary in their disease resistance. Since all bloom well, we chose ones for great fruit display and disease resistance. In spring, the white blossoms of *M*. 'David', 'Donald Wyman', 'Jewelberry', and 'Snowdrift' dominate the planting, with splashes of fiery pink from 'Indian Summer' and the burgundy foliage of *Acer palmatum* 'Bloodgood'. Underneath the trees are rivers of naturalized daffodils and other bulbs. In autumn, the red crabapple fruits last several months until finally being eaten by birds.

Crataegus viridis 'Winter King' grows in the lower part of the Orchard. It is magnificent with its white flowers in the spring, clean green leaves in summer, and a strong show of orangey red fruit in the fall. A beautiful pair of 'Winter King' hawthorns flanks the Chanticleer

TOP   Purple, pealike pods supplant the flower clusters of giant redbud (*Cercis gigantea*) near the Entrance Pavilion.

BOTTOM   Their susceptibility to disease and pests has cast crabapples out of horticultural favor, yet we cannot be without their spring beauty and carefully select only disease- and pest-resistant cultivars. One favorite, *Malus* 'Snowdrift', is a dense crown of powder white flowers that magically hovers over the Orchard's naturalized white daffodils.

Terraces. Horizontal branches hold the brilliant fruit into winter, when hungry birds devour them. Apparently the fruits are not tasty till then.

Magnolias have the biggest flowers of the spring-flowering trees, which also means they look the worst when hit by spring frosts. Tolerant of sun or shade, they bloom best in full sun. Asian species are the first to bloom, putting on amazing displays before leaves expand. Unfortunately, this early flowering exposes the blossoms to frost, which turns them into brown crepe paper. Star magnolia (*Magnolia stellata*) and its hybrid Loebner magnolia (*M. ×loebneri*) are the first to bloom, with narrow, white petals (technically tepals). Yulan magnolias (*M. denudata*) by the Ruin bloom white with wider tepals in early spring. Its offspring, saucer magnolia (*M. ×soulangeana*), has similar blossoms but pink in color. These magnolia blossoms are all fragrant.

Yellow-flowered magnolias have *Magnolia acuminata* var. *subcordata* in their parentage; it is a mid-spring-blooming American native. The later bloom time of yellow magnolias makes them unlikely to be hit by frost. The most famous is 'Elizabeth', and four large plants straddle the path in the lower Orchard slope, near two other yellow magnolias, 'Judy Zuk' and 'Lois'. All three were hybridized at the Brooklyn Botanic Garden, so we jokingly call this our Brooklyn corner. Judy Zuk lived at Chanticleer for seven years before she became president of the Brooklyn Botanical Garden. Her eponymous tree is the last of the Brooklyn magnolias to bloom, with flowers and leaves appearing together in late spring.

Several other native magnolias bloom even later. *Magnolia acuminata*, growing above the Serpentine, has green flowers that appear in late spring. Beautiful and clearly magnolialike in shape, the flowers are so camouflaged you have to look closely to find them. Nearby and in Asian Woods is bigleaf magnolia, *M. macrophylla*, whose Latin and English names are totally descriptive. It features 2-foot-long leaves and big white flowers in late spring. *Magnolia macrophylla* subsp. *ashei* has equally large leaves and flowers, but on a smaller tree, and blooms at a young age, sometimes when only five years old and 3 feet tall.

Cornus florida, flowering dogwood, is the crown jewel of eastern North American forests and may be our most-loved native plant. Its large, white bracts are showy for three weeks in mid-spring just as its leaves are expanding. Flowering dogwood is planted throughout Chanticleer, but the oldest specimen is in the Teacup Garden, commanding admiration. The nearby iron railing has dogwood blossoms included in the design, as does the Teacup fountain itself. Its Asian cousin *C. kousa* blooms a month later and remains showy for at least a month. A specimen on the path below the Apple House is a favorite of our guests. The bracts of both species turn pink as they fade. Both dogwoods thrive in sun and shade and have reddish orange autumn foliage color.

Fringe tree is another genus with American and Asian species. The American *Chionanthus virginicus* is a multistemmed small tree or

Guests sometimes mistake the pair of hawthorns (*Crataegus viridis* 'Winter King') flanking the Chanticleer Terraces for crabapples.

LEFT   The flowers of *Magnolia* 'Elizabeth' start a strong yellow and then fade to white, betraying its Yulan magnolia heritage.

RIGHT   The silvery undersides of a *Magnolia macrophylla* leaf remain vivid even when shed onto the ground. This species looks tropical because of its bold, large leaves, seemingly unlikely in a temperate climate.

Magnolia 'Lois' is wider spreading in habit than 'Elizabeth' and is another Brooklyn Botanic Garden hybrid.

The fruits of *Cornus kousa* and *C. florida* demonstrate ecological divergences: Primates feast on the former's raspberrylike berries, whereas birds feed on the latter's drupes. The two dogwoods are beautiful ornamental trees worthy of any garden.

Cornus kousa

Cornus florida

Dwarfing the Spring House, white fringe tree (*Chionanthus virginicus*) is happy in the Pond Garden's moist soil.

large shrub with light, airy white blossoms that appear in mid-spring when the leaves are emerging. Found in several places here, including the Creek Garden and Bell's Woodland, it tolerates damp to dry soil, sun and shade, but blooms best in the sun. A small grove of its Asian cousin, *C. retusus*, grows next to the Serpentine basins. The showy white flowers appear slightly later than for the American species, with wider spreading branches, shiny dark green leaves, and rougher bark. A *C. retusus* specimen is espaliered at the Ruin.

SHRUBS

Shrubs are extremely useful plants in the garden because they are visually and functionally between trees and herbaceous plants in height. They are versatile, serving as screens, lending winter interest to herbaceous areas, and adding color to the garden through their leaves, flowers, and fruits.

Evergreen Shrubs for Screening and Ornament

Evergreen shrubs function in areas where a smaller size is needed. Often there isn't room for a tall tree for screening, or the screening needs to be shorter. Evergreen shrubs drop some leaves but not all of the leaves at once.

Rhododendrons are probably the best known flowering evergreen shrubs. *Rhododendron maximum*, *R. catawbiense*, *R. minus*, and their hybrids are East Coast natives with attractive foliage and flowers. You'll find them on the Wildflower Slope, in Minder Woods, and in Bell's Woodland. Like all members of the genus, they grow best in light shade with well-drained soil that is never dry. The last of the evergreen rhododendrons to bloom here is *R. maximum*. This Pennsylvania native has purplish pink flowers and blooms in late spring/early summer. It has large leaves and grows to 12 feet high and wide, making it a useful screening shrub. Similarly leaved false daphne (*Daphniphyllum macropodum*), another evergreen shrub, shows off in Asian Woods. It grows more upright than rhododendrons, with small flowers and reddish petioles, and deer do not eat it. For a comparable effect but with larger red flowers and fragrant leaves, try Florida anise (*Illicium floridanum*). These two genera need to grow in shade and out of the wind.

Small-leaved, evergreen rhododendrons tend to be smaller shrubs and fit more easily into small spaces. 'Mary Fleming' welcomes guests at the Entrance with its pinkish yellow flowers in mid-spring and brightens Minder Woods as an understory planting. It was bred by Guy Nearing in his nearby Guyencourt Nurseries in Delaware. We've used 'Dora Amateis' in containers on the Chanticleer Terraces. At 3 feet tall, it is the perfect size for a large container. The deep green leaves are attractive throughout the season after the bright white flowers are finished. We haven't checked the root hardiness on either of these plants, but we suspect 'Mary Fleming' would overwinter successfully in a container.

Mountain laurel (*Kalmia latifolia*), a stunningly beautiful evergreen shrub, is the state flower of Pennsylvania. It covers many of Pennsylvania's mountainsides, growing in sun and shade. Unfortunately, we've had difficulty establishing young plants in the garden, perhaps because of a lack of mycorrhizal association. Mycorrhizae are symbiotic fungi that have been found to be helpful in the growth of roots.

Deer find the alkaloid-laden leaves of false daphne (*Daphniphyllum macropodum*) poisonous, making this rhododendron doppelganger an excellent choice for heavily browsed gardens. An evergreen Asian native, it is a tall understory shrub in Asian Woods.

Rhododendron 'English Roseum' graces the corner of the Chanticleer House garage, with the similarly rosy-hued *Weigela florida* 'Variegata' to the left. 'English Roseum' inherited from its parent, *Rhododendron catawbiense*, excellent hardiness, vigor, and large trusses of rosy flowers.

A mature specimen of mountain laurel (*Kalmia latifolia*) blooms in full glory near the Waterwheel.

A grouping of holly (*Ilex crenata* 'Sky Pencil') passes for a set of ebony obelisks near the Ruin's water table, while the golden autumn color of *Hydrangea anomala* subsp. *petiolaris* glows in the background.

The plum yew (genus *Cephalotaxus*) has received attention because deer rarely eat it. *Cephalotaxus harringtonii* 'Prostrata' and 'Duke Gardens' are handsome low shrubs in the Parking Lot Garden. 'Prostrata' is a shorter shrub with downward pointing branches; it was the recipient of a Gold Medal from the Pennsylvania Horticultural Society. The tips of the branches of 'Duke Gardens' are more horizontal, pointing slightly upward. *Cephalotaxus harringtonii* 'Fastigiata' is narrow as a young plant, with whorled foliage, becoming vase-shaped with age. We've used it at the Ruin for its wall-like quality, but we now have to prune it to keep it narrow.

Nearby, even more effective as a wall, is an even tighter upright plant: *Ilex crenata* 'Sky Pencil'. This holly species has small, boxwood-like, alternate leaves (boxwood's are opposite). Also at the Ruin, an upright box, *Buxus sempervirens* 'Dee Runk', is a narrow pyramid with a central leader ('Sky Pencil' is multistemmed) and a wider base. The adjective "clipped" comes to mind with boxwood. We use *B.* 'Green Velvet' in tight hedges on the Chanticleer Terraces and the very hardy 'Vardar Valley' unclipped at the nearby swimming pool.

Cherry laurel (*Prunus laurocerasus*) is shrubby, evergreen, and takes full sun and shade. It responds well to heavy pruning, which is useful when the plant is crushed by snow or needs renewal pruning: you can cut the shoots to the ground and they will regrow. Its white flowers are pleasing, but the main reason to use it is for its toughness. Portuguese laurel (*Prunus lusitanica*) is similar with narrower leaves. We're trying it in several areas.

Sweetbox (*Sarcococca hookeriana* var. *humilis*) is low growing, making a 10- to 12-inch ground cover in shaded areas. Its flowers are extremely fragrant but inconspicuous. Guests walking by sarcococca in early spring at the Asian Woods Restrooms notice the wonderful fragrance but can't figure out what plant is producing it. We use it to hide electrical outlets near the Tennis Court, since it is easily woven around the boxes and robust enough to regrow if damaged.

Buxus 'Green Velvet', a cold-hardy boxwood cross between *B. sempervirens* and *B. microphylla* var. *koreana*, performs well as a tight hedge at the Chanticleer Terraces.

Shrubs for Colorful Foliage

Continuing the yellow theme on the Chanticleer Terraces, smokebush (*Cotinus coggygria* 'Golden Spirit') is nestled in the corner of the limestone balustrade. At its flowers' expense, cotinus can be coppiced (cut back hard) in early spring for larger, more colorful leaves.

Shrubs bring added color into perennial beds throughout the growing season. *Weigela florida* 'Variegata' and *Cornus controversa* 'Variegata' have clean white, variegated foliage. Weigela's foliage is complemented with pink flowers in the spring, and the dogwood has strongly horizontal, tiered architecture and white flowers in June. *Cornus alternifolia* 'Golden Shadows' is similar to *C. controversa*, but with yellow variegation and thinner twigs. It is slower growing and less tolerant of hot conditions.

Purple leaves powerfully contrast with yellow- and green-leaved plants. We've been impressed with purple-leaved cultivars of *Weigela florida*: 'Elvera', 'Alexandra', and 'Java Red'. *Physocarpus opulifolius* 'Diabolo', a selection of native ninebark, is similar in effect. All are tough plants, surviving most soils, but have the best color in full sun. Ninebarks root easily and are used for bank stabilization: you can stick small shoots directly into the soil in early spring wherever you want a plant. There are many purple-leaved selections of smokebush (*Cotinus coggygria*). Cutting them back hard in the spring keeps them from blooming and doubles the size and effect of the leaves.

A young shoot of smokebush (*Cotinus coggygria*) glows a surreal shade of fluorescent red.

Physocarpus opulifolius 'Dart's Gold' is an attractive yellow-leaved shrub, as are *Cotinus coggygria* 'Golden Spirit', *Sambucus racemosa* 'Sutherland Gold', and *Cercis canadensis* 'Hearts of Gold'; *Cercis canadensis* 'Hearts of Gold' eventually becomes a small tree. These shrubs are used on the Chanticleer Terraces to develop a yellow theme, where the low wall in the center and a terra-cotta pot are covered with *Hedera helix* 'Buttercup', and across on the balustrade, you'll find *Parthenocissus tricuspidata* 'Fenway Park'. The yellow ground plane consists of *Hakonechloa macra* 'Aureola' and is complemented with the blue flowers of *Clematis* ×*durandii* and purple foliage of *Sambucus nigra* 'Black Beauty'.

Deciduous Shrubs

Many shrubs have a cameo role in the garden, stealing the show for several weeks and then blending into the background. Examples are *Weigela* and *Kolkwitzia*, which present showy blossoms in May above the Tennis Court. The flowers are followed by simple green leaves that merely turn brown in autumn. Beauty bush (*Kolkwitzia*) has exfoliating bark on the older stems, providing some winter interest. Selections of *Weigela* with colored leaves extend the colorful period from just days in the spring to a multimonth experience.

The most useful shrubs have multiseasonal interest, with showy flowers and later fruits, fall color, and interesting form in winter. When choosing shrubs, aim for multiseasonal effects; don't be seduced by flowers alone.

Deciduous rhododendrons and azaleas have star quality. They tolerate sun and shade, vary in size, color, and fragrance, and also have autumn color. Combine them and you'll get a long bloom period as well, starting with *Rhododendron periclymenoides* in mid-spring, and all the way into midsummer to late summer with *R. prunifolium* and *R. viscosum* var. *serrulatum*. In Minder Woods, *R. vaseyi* has large pink flowers, as does its Asian counterpart, *R. schlippenbachii* near the arbor. Both bloom in mid-spring, as do the fragrant *R. viscosum* and *R. atlanticum*, both of which tolerate wet soils. For a burst of orange and yellow, we've used *R. calendulaceum*, *R. viscosum* var. *serrulatum*, *R. austrinum*, and their hybrids in the Creek Garden and Wildflower Slope.

Rhododendron mucronulatum announces spring with bright lavender flowers. It pairs beautifully with any species of yellow-blooming winter hazel (*Corylopsis*). *Corylopsis sinensis* has long, dangling clusters of yellow flowers. It towers over the Entrance walkway from a height of 15 feet and spreads to about 12 feet. Smaller in stature, *C. pauciflora* has smaller, lighter yellow flowers. Our espaliered plant in the Ruin brings gasps in the spring. Both *Corylopsis* species turn a golden yellow in autumn.

Viburnums take the crown for multiseason interest in the garden, tolerating sun and shade. Their attractive white flowers are followed by showy fruits and bright fall color. *Viburnum nudum* and *V. cassinoides*

A red-flowering deciduous rhododendron, probably 'Gibraltar', is an electrifying jolt of color by the relatively tranquil pond.

Beauty bush (*Kolkwitzia amabilis*) was once popular in gardens and has recently been rediscovered for its old-fashioned virtues. The light pink, bell-shaped flowers are borne in such profusion that the shrub appears leafless.

Birds surprisingly avoid devouring the orange fruit of *Viburnum setigerum* dangling near the Minder Woods pathway until midwinter.

OPPOSITE   The enormous snowball flowers of *Viburnum macrocephalum* f. *macrocephalum* debut in May.

are planted near the Spring House at the Ponds. These two native species are quite similar, but the southern *V. nudum* has shinier leaves and blooms before the northern *V. cassinoides*. Both have impressive fruit, slowly turning from pink to deep blue, offering an arresting complement to the wine-colored autumn leaves. Asian *V. setigerum* and *V. dilatatum* offer white flowers in the spring, showy red fruits in the fall and early winter, and yellow to orange autumn color.

Native *Viburnum acerifolium* in Bell's Woodland reaches a diminutive 5 feet tall, has small white flowers in 3-inch clusters in mid-spring, and blue-black fruit. Its small, maplelike leaves are pubescent on the underside and turn a rich pink in autumn. *Viburnum trilobum* has similar (but hairless) maple-shaped leaves, but showier white lacecap flower clusters surrounded by larger sterile florets. The drooping clusters of cranberrylike red berries are showy and tasty, if you like sour. It grows 10 to 12 feet tall. *Viburnum dentatum* is a tough native with white flowers, blue-black fruit, and orange autumn color. We used the shorter, heavily fruiting cultivar 'Blue Muffin' in the Parking Lot Garden and on the Long Border.

When we hear of big flower heads, we immediately think of *Viburnum macrocephalum* f. *macrocephalum* (which, if you translate the Latin, means the big-headed form of the big-headed viburnum; love those plant names). The large balls of sterile flowers (often confused with later blooming hydrangeas) appear chartreuse in mid-spring and become creamy white for more than a month of effect. They bloom in the Bulb Meadow along with the spring bulbs. Not a shrub for a small space, it reaches 15 feet tall and 12 feet wide. Blackhaw viburnum (*Viburnum prunifolium*) also reaches large dimensions: It can become a small tree, with white flowers, blue-black fruit, and orange autumn color. It tolerates wet and dry soils and can sucker, forming a thicket.

Hydrangeas are arguably the most spectacular summer-flowering shrubs. They offer a long period of bloom at a time when few shrubs show color. They brighten our days just as summer heat and humidity become tiresome. They excel in shade and will grow in full sun, but quickly wilt in the heat. The Gravel Circle at the Chanticleer House is surrounded by various selections and seedlings of Asian *Hydrangea macrophylla* and *H. serrata*. *Hydrangea serrata* has smaller leaves and flowers than *H. macrophylla*. We've painted the chairs in the circle hydrangea blue to capture the feeling of the plants throughout our open season.

These hydrangeas famously vary their color depending on the pH of the soil (alkaline soils yield pink, acid soils yield blue), and produce flowers on buds formed the previous season (on old wood). Pruning at any time removes flower buds, so we only remove old stems, cut at ground level, usually taking out no more than a quarter of the stems. We remove the old flower heads in the winter, taking care to not cut off buds. Hardiness is also an issue, in that if there is winter dieback, there will be no blooms, so we try to choose selections of proven cold-hardiness.

We use a mixture of colors and flower types around the Gravel Circle for an informal feeling. Some cultivars are more likely to have a consistent flower color regardless of soil pH. *Hydrangea macrophylla* 'Nachtigall' and *H. serrata* 'Miyama Yae Murasaki' are our prettiest blues. 'Nachtigall' has blue, lacecap flowers (a circle of showy sterile flowers surrounding a center of smaller, fertile flowers). In the case of 'Miyama Yae Murasaki', the sterile flowers are double, with more than twice the usual number of petals. It is a crowd-pleaser near the Asian Woods Restrooms. *Hydrangea serrata* 'Blue Billow' is the hardiest of our blue-blooming hydrangeas but not as showy. *Hydrangea* 'Preziosa' blooms pink and fades to maroon, contrasting stunningly with the raked gravel at Chanticleer House. In our memory, it has never missed a year of bloom and is showy from midsummer till frost. All of its flowers are sterile, resulting in an impressive ball of flowers. Hydrangea blossoms fade to tan in winter and are attractive dried.

Native smooth hydrangea (*Hydrangea arborescens*) blooms on new wood, meaning you can cut the entire plant to the ground in the spring and it will still bloom that season. It has delicate, small, white fertile flowers, with only a few sterile flowers. *Hydrangea arborescens* subsp. *radiata* is a little showier in flower, and its leaves have an attractive silvery underside. It grows just outside the Gravel Circle at the base of a column. *Hydrangea arborescens* 'Annabelle' has big heads of white sterile flowers that are showy for most of the summer. The heavy flower clusters often weigh down the plants, as can be seen in the Parking Lot Garden, where they also wilt in the summer sun. 'Incrediball' smooth hydrangea has flower heads almost twice as big.

Hydrangea macrophylla 'Blue Wave', the archetypical lacecap hydrangea, has large ray flowers encircling the tiny center flowers.

Nothing beats the midsummer kaleidoscopic colors of hydrangeas around the Gravel Circle.

Blue chairs imprinted with *Aesculus* nuts and leaves take after the intense blue *Hydrangea macrophylla* 'Endless Summer'.

OPPOSITE   Out of the few dozen hydrangeas we grow, *Hydrangea* 'Preziosa' is unmatched for its brilliant flowers, beautiful foliage that turns a fall burgundy color, and solid hardiness. When a cold winter obliterates the summer display for most *H. macrophylla*, 'Preziosa' sails through to deliver the goods.

Native oak-leaf hydrangea (*Hydrangea quercifolia*) has pyramidal panicles of a mix of sterile and fertile flowers on plants about 6 feet tall. Its large buds and exfoliating bark, along with tan old flowers, make the plant attractive in winter as well as in summer. Autumn color is a rusty orange. Although it will bloom on new wood, the best floral (and bark) display comes from infrequent pruning. *Hydrangea paniculata* is best known through its cultivars, some early blooming, others late. 'Praecox' is the first to bloom, with a pyramidal mixture of sterile and fertile flowers. Like all members of this species, it blooms on new wood, can be pruned hard to achieve a shrubby effect (about 6 feet high), or can be trained as a small tree, reaching 15 to 20 feet. The flowers fade from white to pink and finally to tan. Most of the other cultivars bloom a bit later, including 'Limelight' (with a chartreuse cast to the flowers), 'Pink Diamond' (pinkish), and the sterile 'Grandiflora' (which we do

Hydrangea paniculata 'Quick Fire' at the Ruin Meadow lives up to its billing, because the white panicles quickly turn burgundy shortly after the true flowers finish. It flowers at least a month earlier than other cultivars of the species but benefits from the same pruning regime.

OPPOSITE   Light frost outlines the jagged leaf edges of *Hydrangea quercifolia*.

Pruning Shrubs

Renewal pruning of shrubs offers the promise of eternal youth for the plants. Remove old shoots to encourage growth of new, young shoots where you make the cut. When pruning a shrub, look first to the biggest shoot you can take out, and if possible, take out the entire shoot at ground level. It takes some courage to do this, but new shoots will arise from the base, with no ugly stubs to view. The best time for this pruning is in the winter, when you can see the shape of the plant. Vigorous spring growth will quickly fill in any hole left in the plant.

not have). 'Tardiva' is last to bloom, in midsummer to late summer, and can be seen above the Tennis Court. Most hydrangeas propagate easily from rooted cuttings, and sometimes you'll be successful merely sticking cut shoots directly in the ground in late winter.

Shrubs in Perennial Flower Beds

We mix shrubs into many perennial areas to lend height, winter interest, and structure. In the Pond Garden, Joe Henderson used a number of grounsel shrubs (*Baccharis halimifolia*). This plant is dioecious, meaning it has different sexes on different plants. Female plants are showier, having larger flowers followed by fluffy white seed heads that float about and create a truly magical experience (but may become weedy). Joe is eliminating the males and hoping the lonely females will produce sterile seeds and so not be weedy. Grounsel is a large shrub, growing 8 to 12 feet tall, but it fits well with the large space and plants of the Ponds.

In the Gravel Garden, dwarf hemlocks, 'Emerald Sentinel' junipers, and tree yuccas contribute color, structure, and interest to the winter herbaceous landscape. *Yucca rostrata* is the hardiest of the trunk-forming yuccas and creates an evergreen sphere of gray-blue, spiky (but not sharp) foliage. The Tennis Court uses spireas (*Spiraea nipponica* 'Snowmound', *S.* ×*bumalda* 'Fire Light' and 'Magic Carpet', and *S. thunbergii* 'Ogon') mixed with herbaceous perennials. These low, yellow-leaved shrubs lend color and fine texture throughout the gardening season. Their flowers are bonuses rather than central features.

Deciduous hollies are known for their autumn fruit display, which shines as the leaves drop. Selections of winterberry, *Ilex verticillata*, perform in the Creek Garden, Bell's Woodland, and Parking Lot Garden. A native of wetlands, it grows in wet or dry conditions, sun or shade. 'Winter Red' holds its fruits the longest, into the spring. 'Sparkleberry' is a hybrid, having smaller yet showy fruit. As with any holly, the females fruit but males are needed for pollination. The cultivar 'Southern Gentleman' is an excellent pollinator choice.

We wait until late winter to remove the dried hydrangea seed heads because they become structural garden accents especially when dusted with snow.

Rather inconspicuous for much of the year, *Baccharis halimifolia* explodes onto the scene in late autumn by offering tufts of white seed heads throughout the Pond Garden.

GIVING THE EYE
A CHANCE TO REST

Chanticleer's plantings are designed to stimulate the senses, but if every square inch of the garden's acreage were planted the way the Tennis Court and the Pond Garden are, the garden would not be a relaxing place to visit. The senses need time to rest.

Lawns

Lawns are a significant design feature at Chanticleer. Grasses are an important counterpart to the exuberant color of the garden. They serve as visual rest stops as you travel from one garden room to another. They are wonderful to walk and roll on, and soften the overall feel of the place. They control erosion, filter rainwater, and provide a porous surface, reducing storm water runoff. Scott Steinfeldt and our talented grounds crew give turf (or lawns) the same kind of care the horticulturists give the other plants. Most of our lawns are maintained at what we consider a "medium" level and planted with turf-type tall fescue, which tolerates foot traffic, cold winters, and hot summers. Once established, this fescue has a drought-tolerant, deep root system and resists most diseases. We overseed the lawns in mid-August to mid-September, a better time for seed germination than spring.

We design our lawn maintenance program to reduce plant stress, encourage strong turf, and be environmentally friendly—all practices applicable to home lawns. We cut at 3 to 4 inches, removing no more than one-third of a grass blade in a mowing. Cutting shorter stresses the grass, requiring more water and fertilizer. We keep our mower blades sharp, reducing disease encouraged by torn and bruised grass blades.

The Great Lawn west of the Chanticleer House is a major view spot and a favorite for rolling down. Facing southwest, this slope receives sunlight most of the day and is extra dry since it's at the top of a hill. When we have cistern-captured water available, we use it for supplemental irrigation. In times of drought, the grass goes dormant and tan, recovering when rains return. To reduce water stress, we mow at a height of 3½ inches in the spring and fall and 4 inches during the summer. White clover has seeded itself into this lawn, growing wherever the grass is weak. We allow the clover to grow, enriching the soil with its deep, nitrogen-fixing roots, and it is a favorite to honey bees.

Scott fertilizes based on soil sampling and soil biology reports from our local cooperative extension office. The reports show what is lacking in the soil and list recommendations for correcting deficiencies in order to promote a healthy turf grass system. We use organic-based fertilizers, annually applying 2 to 2.5 pounds of nitrogen (spread in three applications) for every 1,000 square feet. Organic fertilizers help

TOP   The Great Lawn is loved for its green openness, which seems to invite children of any age to roll in the grass.

BOTTOM   Because of their visual importance, the Chanticleer Terrace lawns receive more mollycoddling than other turf areas in the garden.

maintain the soil's carbon reserve and provide a food source for beneficial microorganisms.

The Chanticleer Terrace lawns are an exception, receiving a higher degree of maintenance. We cut the lawn to a height of 2 inches twice a week and edge each time for a crisp, clean appearance. This site has an irrigation system, and is watered when necessary to meet the needs of the microclimate in this area. The area is south-facing and surrounded by paving, so its temperature is several degrees warmer than at our other lawns. If there are no rains, we apply about 1 inch of water a week, watering between 5 and 8 a.m. Early morning watering minimizes evaporation, allowing the water to efficiently penetrate the soil and the leaves to dry before evening, reducing fungal issues.

Meadows

As wonderful as lawns are, there are alternatives—other ways to give the senses a rest and the eyes room to roam that don't require the same level of maintenance. Meadows incorporate longer grass than lawns, but a mixed meadow with flowers as well as grasses can be thought of as a wild perennial bed. There is no clear distinction between the two, although a perennial bed is expected to be well weeded and a meadow is not. The Pond Garden could be described as a well-ordered meadow or an overly exuberant perennial bed.

On the Chanticleer Terraces, we converted an area of turf to a "flowery lawn." The "lawn" grass is a mixture of fine-leaf fescues, mowed annually in November to a height of 4½ inches. These fescues naturally mound to an effective height of about 8 inches. Spring bulbs and summer annuals are dotted throughout, and the area becomes alive with butterflies and other pollinators. We frame the flowery lawn with cut turf.

Perhaps our most photographed meadow is the one at the Ruin. It consists of prairie dropseed grass (*Sporobolus heterolepis*), which is beautiful in every season. We planted the grass in plugs spaced about 18 inches apart. Mulch kept down the weeds until the plants fully filled in after three years. Originally we mowed the grass every winter, but now the local fire department burns it in late winter. The controlled burn takes about 45 minutes; uncontrolled, it would take 5 minutes. Burning rejuvenates the plants, leaving dramatic black clumps and a lingering fiery smell. Within a few weeks, the black pincushion shapes sprout green, and by mid-spring, the area is fully vegetated. In summer, the long leaves appear relaxed and seem to invite one to roll in them. By late summer, the plants bloom and produce a hard-to-describe fragrance (perhaps cilantro-flavored popcorn?). Autumn turns the plants orange-tan, and by winter they are fully tan. The visual impact of the mass of prairie dropseed is so striking we've kept it to a monoculture, inserting only a few other plants.

TOP The flowery lawn was once a mown panel of turf surrounding a central stone patio.

BOTTOM It is hard not to compare the rain-laden tussocks of prairie dropseed grass (*Sporobolus heterolepis*) in the Ruin Meadow to piles of strewn seaweed along ocean beaches.

Low morning light accentuates the textural contrast between long grass and mown grass. The long grass defines the outlines of the Orchard's planting beds as well as hiding the maturing bulb foliage.

We use fine fescues in other areas where we want the effect of low, rough grass. The metasequoias at the Entrance are underplanted with a rough turf of fine fescue. We mow it annually in late autumn. In the bulb lawns of the Orchard, Bulb Meadow, and Creek Garden, turf grass grows long while the bulb foliage ripens, then we mow it at the beginning of summer. Some areas are mowed weekly during the rest of the summer, and in other sections, the grass grows long again and is cut to about 5 inches every six weeks. Turf allowed to grow long becomes mixed with other plants, including weeds that require hand-weeding.

In a few sections, we simply don't cut the turf grass. These areas mirror the outline of planting beds as well as frame lawn areas, changing the focus of the eye. This concept works well for lawns of any size: just mark out a shape or design and let the grass grow unmown. The contrast between mowed and unmowed is beautiful, especially in late-evening sunlight. It's best to cut the longer grass a few times during the season to reduce the number of broad-leaved weeds and tree seedlings. We usually mow these areas twice a season, with mowers raised to 5 inches. Alternatively, we use a string trimmer to cut the grass. In either case, we cut when the grass is dry and remove the debris.

Just below the Serpentine is a bed of Pennsylvania sedge (*Carex pensylvanica*). It reaches 6 to 8 inches in height, and resembles fine fescue but is more yellowish green and less mounding. The sedge spreads by rhizomes and forms a solid mat. It is evergreen, but by spring is a bit tattered, so we mow it once to about 4 inches. It tolerates sun and shade as well as wet and dry conditions.

A New Look at Lawns

PETER BRINDLE

For decades, we mowed most Chanticleer grassy areas each week . . . well, just because they had always been mowed each week. More recently, we began to question whether there was a good reason for this approach. We could see the beauty of meadows across the road on the dairy farm, so we began to allow some selected perimeter areas to go unmown. It saves on noise, fuel, machinery wear, pollution, and labor, and looks more interesting. The long grass softens odd corners and nooks, and deters visitors from walking into perimeter areas by guiding their eyes and feet. Over time, we have taken a couple of acres out of the weekly mowing equation, and a simple mowed verge alongside the tall grass sends the message this was all intentional. Of course, our gardeners know an opportunity when they see one. Soon, meadowy wild flowers and bulbs began springing up in the tall grass, softening the entire garden and enhancing the visual flow.

Perhaps there's a bigger life lesson in all this? It occurred to me the other day that the lawn at the Chanticleer Terraces was probably mowed each week for ninety-nine years before Jonathan came up with the idea of a flowery lawn.

Several mowings a year control the broad-leaved weeds and tree seedlings in the long grass.

The first rays of morning sunlight spotlight *Sporobolus heterolepis* in full bloom.

Water Features and Water Plants

Like lawns and meadows, water areas in the garden give the senses a break and allow the eye to see distances. Running water is dynamic, lending sound while attracting birds and other wildlife. Chanticleer's water features run the gamut from ponds to creeks (large, small, and seasonal), a swimming pool and several reflecting pools, fountains, a waterwheel, and even water-filled pots.

Water is reflective and meditative, and it physically cools its surroundings. The Ponds are full of life, including turtles that swim with the catfish, bluegills, and colorful koi. Hawks, herons, kingfishers, ducks, occasional geese, songbirds, wrens, and goldfinches patrol the air, while snakes (none poisonous) and frogs add excitement on the ground and in the water.

The largest (and lowest) of our five ponds is clay-lined, fed by springs and water siphoned from Bell's Run, and was built along with the picturesque Spring House in the 1970s. Adolph Jr. kept the lawn around the pond mowed. Beginning in the 1990s, Joe Henderson added more ponds and heavily planted the edges as well as the water itself. Several cultivars of water lilies grow in these serene waters, with leaves lying flat on the water's surface, hiding fish from predators. Our water lilies are hardy as long as the crown of the plant is below the ice line of the ponds. Year-round pumps keep the water from freezing solid. *Nymphaea* 'Texas Dawn' has mottled leaves and large, fragrant, lemon-yellow flowers. 'Arc-en-Ciel' has fragrant pink flowers fading to white with yellow centers. 'James Brydon' has purple-tinged leaves with large, double, fragrant cerise-red flowers with yellow centers. 'Pygmaea Helvola', a miniature water lily, is perfect in a small pond. It has creamy yellow flowers, and we grow it in a container near the Spring House.

Our guests' favorite water plant is lotus (*Nelumbo*). Its leaves start on the water's surface, and, as the summer warms, rise above the water. By midsummer, the big 10-inch, pink-tipped, cream flowers of 'Mrs. Perry D. Slocum' break open with a scent of cola, with enormous, blue-green leaves visible from the Chanticleer Terraces. Water-repellant, the leaves fill with rain in storms, then sway and dump the beads of moisture. The attractive seed heads look like old-fashioned showerheads and nod as winter hits.

This sterile hybrid (native *Nelumbo lutea* crossed with Asian *N. nucifera*) is extremely vigorous. Joe digs out some of the growth several times a year to prevent it from filling the pond. From a rowboat, he uses a Chanticleer-made tool of three downward-facing prongs mounted on a long pole. With a twist and a tug, he dislodges the rapidly expanding new growth. Lotuses winterkill if their growing shoots freeze. Our ponds are deep, so the roots and shoots are buried safely in a couple of feet of mud below a few feet of water. To echo the lotus on land, we cut a princess tree (*Paulownia tomentosa*) to the ground each winter.

We annually field phone calls about when lotuses will bloom and it's easy to see why. The sumptuous *Nelumbo* 'Mrs. Perry D. Slocum' has a magnetic appeal for visitors.

With coloration suggestive of its namesake, *Nymphaea* 'Texas Dawn' has the same floral stamina as tropical water lilies but survives our winters. Its lemon-scented flowers appear from summer to autumn.

It reflushes in the spring with huge leaves to rival those of the lotus. *Nelumbo* 'Momo Botan' is a dwarf lotus cultivar and easier to use in home gardens. It grows 1 to 2 feet tall with 4- to 10-inch leaves. We use it in containers where we can enjoy its smaller flowers and seed heads. It will survive in ponds and is less aggressive than its larger cousin.

Narrowleaf cattail (*Typha angustifolia*) rises 6 feet in the shallow waters of the lower pond. Red-winged blackbirds build their nests in the previous season's cattail foliage, staking out their territory in early spring. Because of this behavior, Joe doesn't cut back all the old shoots but lets some stand. *Typha minima* is less aggressive and more diminutive, and therefore better suited to small ponds than its aggressive cousin. Hardy *Thalia dealbata* has cannalike, blue-green foliage rising 6 feet above the water, with trusses of small purple flowers. *Thalia* can be top-heavy if grown in containers, so the container should be weighted with stones.

New Jersey Pine Barrens native golden club, *Orontium aquaticum*, is a low, showy, spring bloomer with brilliant white and gold flowers. It grows in shallow water or in wet marginal areas. Variegated sweet flag, *Acorus calamus* 'Variegatus', stands over 2 feet tall in the wet and dry margins of the lower pond. Its bright yellow-cream leaves work well with the pale yellow *Narcissus* 'Hawera'. *Carex stricta* is finer textured, with a light green color, softening the edge of the pond with its mounds of foliage. In the wild, it forms tussocks that stand above shallow water with a petticoat of last year's leaves at the base. Another sedge, *C. riparia* 'Variegata', emerges in the spring with erect, white leaves and contrasting black seed heads. Later, the variegation matures to solid green. Older plants may mutate green and become aggressively weedy, so we remove any green shoots in the spring.

Water plantain (*Alisma subcordatum*) yields a constellation of tiny flowers over its wide, green leaves. An obligate wetland plant (meaning it must grow in wet areas), it thrives along the damp clay banks of the lowest pond. Bold-leaved Indian rhubarb (*Darmera peltata*) produces attractive pink flowers before the leaves in spring, followed by rough-textured, roundish leaves growing from a slithering mass of rhizomes creeping above wet soil. In partial shade, the leaves grow to a height of 3 feet; in full sun, they are a more modest 18 to 24 inches with occasional burned leaves. *Astilboides tabularis* is similar, but with smooth, larger leaves and a plume of white flowers. It is more challenging to grow; our best one is in a moist area by the Waterwheel. Grassleaf sweet flag (*Acorus gramineus* 'Ogon') is a clumping plant with bright yellow and green striped thin, pointed leaves. The leaves persist through the winter, but are a bit weatherworn in the spring, so we cut them to about 3 inches. A great plant for rain gardens, we use 'Ogon' in the seasonal stream in Asian Woods, where it gets occasionally inundated during rains and then tolerates dryness when the rains cease. Best with light shade, it also grows in regular garden soil, doing well on the Long Border.

The bold leaves of *Thalia dealbata* emerge from the water, complementing the landside herbaceous mix of *Patrinia scabiosifolia*, *Eutrochium maculatum* 'Gateway', and *Vernonia novaboracensis*.

Watercress (*Nasturtium officinalis*) grows in shallow, moving water in the creek. Its hollow stems float on the water's surface, with shiny, compound leaves and small, white clustered flowers. Touted as a health wonder food, it has a tangy peppery flavor, similar to that of its relatives mustard and radish. This naturalized marginal (growing in wettish soils) is fast-growing and can crowd out native vegetation, but it is easily pulled.

Narrowleaf cattail (*Typha angustifolia*) is a classic aquatic plant.

Golden club (*Orontium aquaticum*) is one of the earliest flowering aquatic plants, with white "clubs" seemingly dipped in yellow.

Native to streamsides and moist woodlands from southern Oregon to northern California, Indian rhubarb (*Darmera peltata*) has bold, dimpled leaves up to 24 inches wide, preceded by leafless clusters of pinkish white flowers in spring. Clumps are established along the periphery of the Ponds and Bell's Run Creek.

VINES AND CLIMBERS

Vines are flexible (literally and figuratively), vertical elements adding another dimension to garden design. They climb in various ways, are favorite nesting sites for birds, and lend a wildness to a garden. That same wildness is alarming if the wrong vines are chosen or if no control is used with vigorous vines.

Climbing hydrangeas (*Hydrangea anomala* subsp. *petiolaris*, *Schizophragma integrifolium*, *S. hydrangeoides*, and *Decumaria barbara*) cling by aerial roots and freely climb trees in Asian Woods and Bell's Woodland, on stones at the Ruin, and on stucco walls near the Entrance Pavilion. When in bloom, the plants (and therefore anything they are on) are covered in white flowers. The vines grow tightly against the structure until blooming age, when they produce flowers on horizontal shoots. Don't cut these off or you'll never have flowers. These deciduous vines become open in winter, unlike evergreen English ivy, which grows so dense it will conceal structural flaws. *Decumaria* is semievergreen but usually leafless by spring.

Climbing hydrangeas grow slowly for the first three to five years and then become vigorous. Aerial roots allow them to climb tree trunks, and usually they will not girdle trees the way wisteria and bittersweet will. They are easily propagated by taking cuttings of shoots that already have aerial roots. Simply put the cuttings where you want the plant to grow. There is no advantage to buying large plants because existing shoots will never attach to a structure; only new shoots will.

Hydrangea anomala subsp. *petiolaris* blooms first with its small, fertile flowers encircled by four-petal sterile flowers. *Hydrangea anomala* subsp. *petiolaris* 'Firefly', found as a chance mutation by Dan Benarcik, grows slowly because of its yellow variegated foliage. 'Brookside Littleleaf' is a dwarf slow-grower with small leaves. Hydrangea vine (*Schizophragma*) blooms two weeks later and is distinguished by having single bracts surrounding the flowers. *Schizophragma integrifolium* climbs a large dogwood in the Teacup Garden and blooms just after the dogwood, effectively extending its bloom season. *Schizophragma hydrangeoides* 'Moonlight' has silvery leaves, adding a distinctive foliage display, and 'Roseum' has pink bracts. Native climbing hydrangea (*Decumaria barbara*), at the Ruin and in Bell's Woodland, has deep green, shiny leaves and fragrant, small white flowers opening in early summer, the last of the climbing hydrangeas to bloom.

Clematis is called the queen of vines because of its notable flowers. The genus has many wonderful plants and very few bad ones. Clematis vines climb by wrapping their compound leaves around other plants, thin lattice, wires, and mesh, but not masonry. *Clematis* 'Duchess of Albany' has deep pink flowers that only partially open, adding life to the wrought-iron vines of the railings near the Entrance Pavilion. *Clematis* 'Gravetye Beauty' is similar, but a deeper red. Large-flowered,

Chinese hydrangea vine (*Schizophragma integrifolium*) clings via aerial roots and covers itself with white flowers in midsummer.

white *C.* 'Henryi' climbs an arch in the Cut Flower Garden, blooms best with no pruning, and makes a good cut flower, as do most clematis species. *Clematis ×durandii* has attractive blue flowers, but sprawls rather than climbs, reflecting its parent *C. integrifolia*, a 3-foot-high perennial. Its other parent is the large-flowered *C.* 'Jackmanii'. *Clematis* 'Etoile Violette' has 3-inch purple flowers appearing in June and sporadically through the rest of the summer. A hybrid with *C. viticella* as a parent, it is delicate yet floriferous. Removing the spent flowers encourages rebloom, but the golden fruits are also attractive.

Typically, American native clematis species have small but exquisite flowers. Most are not very vigorous and require little pruning. *Clematis glaucophylla*, *C. addisonii*, *C. crispa*, and *C. viorna* have small, fused petals and are best planted where they can be seen close up. *Clematis texensis* is similar, but the flowers are a showier red outlined in yellow. *Clematis virginiana* blooms with a mass of fragrant small, white flowers in late summer and is a perfect substitute for the invasive Asian sweet autumn clematis. You can prune both very hard in the spring since they bloom on new wood.

Our most common native vine is Virginia creeper (*Parthenocissus quinquefolia*) often ignored or considered a weed. We love its blue-black berries and florid red fall color. At the Pond Arbor, Joe Henderson trains it to hang from the top of the arbor in single strands that sway with the breeze like a veil. When backlit, the autumn leaves are stunning. It grows alongside *Wisteria floribunda* 'Shiro Noda', which has amazing 18-inch white racemes of bloom. The Asian wisterias, *W. floribunda* and *W. sinensis*, are extremely vigorous. Don't plant them unless you intend to drastically prune them regularly and have an extremely strong structure for them to climb on. Joe prunes them several times a year to keep the growth in check while producing a scaffold yielding a profusion of bloom. Each time he cuts an errant shoot, he leaves three to five buds.

Two American wisteria species are much less vigorous and easier to use in gardens. They bloom after their leaves flush and have smaller flower clusters than the showy Asians but are beautiful plants. They are hardier, surviving winters north to USDA Zone 5. *Wisteria macrostachya* has longer (to 10 inches) flower clusters than *W. frutescens* (to 6 inches) and is showier. *Wisteria macrostachya* 'Clara Mack' blooms white in late spring near the Entrance, and *W. frutescens* 'Nivea' blooms white on the balustrades on the Chanticleer Terraces. The natural color of both species is purple and can be seen in the Teacup Garden and in Bell's Woodland. All wisterias climb by encircling and do well on columns and posts. They should not be planted on trees because they will eventually girdle them.

Dutchman's pipe (*Aristolochia*) also climbs by twining and has unique flowers that are delightfully weird. The biggest flowers are on the tropical species, and when *A. gigantea* blooms at the Entrance Pavilion, it

Hydrangea anomala subsp. *petiolaris* 'Firefly', a variegated sport discovered by staff horticulturist Dan Benarcik, has half of the typical species' vigor because of its chartreuse-edged leaves. The variegation is the most pronounced in spring, giving the vine a golden aura.

Our native Virginia creeper (*Parthenocissus quinquefolia*) turns a fiery scarlet color in fall, and its inky blue fruits attract the birds.

Clematis 'William Kennett' radiates like a blue-violet sea star among the blossoms of *Rosa* 'Dr. Huey' on a trellis.

The profuse purple racemes of *Wisteria sinensis* 'Amethyst' cover the Gravel Garden Arbor.

Climbing onto trees in Asian Woods, *Aristolochia manshuriensis* shows the distinctive Dutchman's pipe–shaped flowers that give it its common name.

Vines

JOE HENDERSON

Vines are underused in gardens, possibly because there is a feeling of wildness about them: "Oh, that wisteria will rip the tree down," and left to its own devices it might. Vines are extremely useful if you know the plant, anticipate its needs, and realize it may be more attractive if restrained.

Clematis, for example, is a fantastic flowering genus with a dynamic range of growth rates, flower color, and shape, but is too often relegated to a mailbox or lamppost. With a little creativity, clematis can visually extend the flowering of a shrub by blooming at a different time, be used as a ground cover, or climb through a tree. I use small cultivars and species in small spaces, and vigorous ones in large areas.

I like the aggressive *Clematis montana* 'Alba', letting it climb through a declining blue spruce and a 'Silver Umbrella' aralia. We would have cut down the spruce by now had it not been a perfect structure for the clematis. I wouldn't turn this vine loose on a small shrub, but where it is, it conceals the spruce's dying lower limbs. Vanilla-scented white flowers cover the plant in mid-spring. The vine blooms on old wood, so prune it hard when it has finished blooming; if you cut it back in the winter, there will be no flowers.

Clematis montana var. *rubens* is not one for the timid since only large spaces can accommodate its vigorous spread. The sight of this deciduous vine completely covered with fragrant pink flowers is a welcome late spring sight after a long winter.

is a crowd-stopper. The large buds look like odd smoking pipes and then open into large, leathery flowers smelling slightly of rotten meat. Our native *A. macrophylla* has tiny yet interesting flowers covered by huge, heart-shaped leaves. These leaves make a grand textural statement on the Tennis Court Arbor. *Aristolochia tomentosa*, at the Ruin and in Bell's Woodland, has smaller, somewhat gray leaves. Its suckering habit makes it a bit weedy. In Asian Woods, *A. manshuriensis* shows its yellow flowers as the leaves emerge and is the showiest of the hardy aristolochias. All species serve as hosts to the larvae of the spectacular pipevine swallowtail butterfly.

There are some interesting annual and perennial vines that yield edible fruit. Beans, squashes, pumpkins, melons, cucumbers, peas, and even tomatoes are annual climbers and sprawlers in the vegetable world. Quick growers, they can be used to fill in areas in less than a month during the summer. Hardy kiwi (*Actinidia arguta*) is a large (to 20 to 30 feet), vigorous twiner producing grape-sized kiwi fruits after autumn frost. The fruits are as delicious as the kiwis of commerce and have the advantage of being hairless and bite-sized. Grapes are perhaps the most famous of edible vines and climb by having their tendrils grab onto something (a string, wire, or another plant). We don't grow any wine or table grapes, but we've trained *Vitis coignetiae* above the Teacup Garden. It is notable for its large 10-inch leaves with exceptional reddish autumn color. *Vitis davidii* is similar in effect, with smaller leaves, and it has stems covered in attractive, soft thorns (they don't hurt).

Emma Seniuk uses cut grapevines to camouflage rebar arches in the Cut Flower Garden. She harvested the pliable stems from her father's property in early spring before they leafed out. The loosely woven, almost fairy-talelike cut vines harden in position and provide a perfect structure for perennial and annual vines to climb. In a similar mode, Przemek Walczak has used old cut vines on the bridge in Bell's Woodland. These 1-inch-thick stems add a touch of the natural to the metal structure and serve as supports for vines such as Dutchman's pipe.

Climbing Roses

Our most effective roses are climbers, which must have support structures (trellis or a shrub) on which to climb. Unfortunately, most climbing roses (*Rosa* spp.) are not repeat bloomers, putting on their show primarily in mid-spring to early summer. *Rosa* 'Climbing Eden' is a fragrant, cabbage-head double that scrambles up the post to the roosters at the Chanticleer House. Near the swimming pool, 'Dr. Huey' is deep red. 'Eglantyne Climbing' is pink and has one of the strongest fragrances of any of our roses. Equally fragrant is 'Madame Grégoire Staechelin', trained on the wall below the Gravel Garden Arbor. 'New Dawn' is a shower of pink at the Tennis Court Arbor and repeats its pink bloom occasionally throughout the summer.

A serendipitous accident, *Rosa* 'Dr. Huey' was the rootstock of a deceased rose and now is a happy pairing with *Clematis* 'William Kennett'. This rose resists many of the pests and diseases that ail its ilk.

The strongly fragrant, pinkish white *Rosa* 'Paul's Himalayan Musk' nearly covers the cedar shake roof of the Spring House near the Pond Garden. Nearby, 'Westerland' climbs within a *Chionanthus virginicus*. Just after the tree finishes bloom, the apricot orange of the rose takes over, giving another period of color to the planting. In Bell's Woodland, *R. setigera* and *R. virginiana*, both natives, sprawl and bloom with pink flowers. These native species show some signs of resistance to rose rosette disease, which is killing roses in this region. Two other native roses we're growing are *R. palustris* and *R. carolina*.

Support in two ways: *Rosa* 'Paul's Himalayan Musk' scampers over the Spring House roof, and the fragrant orange *Rosa* 'Westerland' climbs into a fringe tree.

Espaliers Cover Walls like Vines

Adolph Jr. espaliered trees and shrubs flat against walls and fences. Most of his espaliers no longer exist, but you'll find younger ones throughout the garden. Almost any tree or shrub can be espaliered. Some of the Ruin's walls are covered with espaliers, which from a distance look like vines. *Acer davidii* is the largest, trained against the high wall above the water table, its green, white-striped bark visible near its base. We prune in the winter and in the summer to keep the plants flat. We tie the branches to the wall and loosen the attachments annually.

Winter hazel (*Corylopsis pauciflora*) grows against a nearby wall. The layered spaces between its branches show off the early spring pendulous

With walls that beg for green cloaking, the Ruin is a showroom for espaliered woody plants. *Acer davidii* is on the left, matched by vines on the right.

The fan-shape silhouette of espaliered 'Luscious' pear (*Pyrus communis* 'Luscious') is etched clearly in the autumnal mists shrouding the Cut Flower Garden.

Espaliering was the solution to an unexpected outcome: When *Ginkgo biloba* 'Princeton Sentry' did not fulfill the vision of tight columnar shapes for the Serpentine, we trained the trees into a curvilinear hedge on stilts.

blossoms beautifully, as does the pruning of 'Jet Trail' flowering quince growing through a nearby Ruin window opening. Just outside the Ruin's "library," frosty elm (*Ulmus parvifolia* 'Frosty') mimics a hedge and *Magnolia grandiflora* 'Edith Bogue' is trained against the wall. *Magnolia grandiflora* is borderline hardy for us, so training it against a wall takes advantage of the warmer microclimate of a wall (any but a north-facing wall, that is). We've used *Magnolia grandiflora* 'Little Gem' on the Chanticleer Terraces for a similar effect. Nearby are espaliers of *Cornus kousa*, *Prunus armeniaca* 'Harcot', *Viburnum* ×*pragense*, and *Stachyurus praecox* 'Rubriflorus'. The stachyurus blooms in late winter and the espalier shows off the drooping pink flower clusters. In the Teacup Garden, we've trained *Salix elaeagnos* and *S.* 'Golden Curls' as wall plants, and near the Entrance, the Asian maple *Acer oliverianum* is trained to two wide-spreading branches.

Espaliers do not have to be against walls. At the upper end of the Serpentine, we've trained 'Princeton Sentry' ginkgoes into a flat, tall hedge. These fastigiate (columnar) trees were originally planted to mimic Lombardy poplars. They were not very successful, so we decided to train and prune them horizontally. Douglas Randolph bent the multiple upright stems sideways and tied them to bamboo stakes. At first, they looked like aerial grapevines. Lisa Roper took over the effort and the trees eventually filled in, looking hedgelike. Doug Croft does the pruning now, in a bucket truck and on a ladder, pruning out shoots that grow out too far and tying in more branches. We now have a single-plane, curved hedge serving as a backdrop for the semicircular, stone seating below.

Wires reinforce the tiered structure of apricot (*Prunus armeniaca* 'Harcot') flowering against the swimming pool wall.

FLOWERING BULBS

Bulbs are like ephemerals, producing a major floral display, storing food for the next year, and then going dormant. Like ephemerals, bulbs evolved to avoid dry periods and are best kept dry during the summer with no irrigation. The bulb itself is a large, belowground structure to store food. For bloom the next year, foliage must be allowed to ripen naturally and not be cut back until it turns brown. Interplanting bulbs with other plants conceals dying foliage. While we refer to this group of plants as bulbs, they are more correctly called "geophytes" because the storage structure botanically may actually be a bulb, tuber, corm, or something else.

The best-known bulbs are spring-bloomers, like tulips and daffodils, but some bulbs bloom in summer (lilies) and others in autumn (colchicums). Almost all bulbs can take sun or shade and are perfect for deciduous shade. We use bulbs in beds, wooded areas, and in lawns. In planting beds, we mix spring bulbs with cool-season annuals and early perennials. Sweeps of spring bulbs add bright color while perennials are still dormant.

Most bulbs are best transplanted when dormant. We plant small bulbs with a gardening knife or a bulb planter that removes a plug of turf and soil. For larger bulbs, we use a large gas-powered drill with a 3- to 4-inch auger to efficiently plant large numbers of bulbs. However, adding more bulbs to an existing planting is a challenge. We sometimes divide and transplant bulbs while in leaf to fill in gaps, extending the planting while we can see the existing bulbs. We also overwinter new bulbs in flats in a cold frame or outside and heavily mulched (under wire mesh to discourage rodents). In spring, we carefully pull apart the bulbs and plant them where we want them to go in an existing planting. We treat bulbs for containers in a similar way, planting them in plastic pots to overwinter in cold frames, and then sinking the pot into a decorative container in the spring.

Tulips are the quintessential spring bulb. The largest flowered tulips are short-lived hybrids, and new cultivars are introduced each year. We use them on the Chanticleer Terraces, and extend the bloom season by mixing early, mid-, and late-flowering cultivars. Darwin tulips are the longest lived of the large-flowered hybrids and have perennialized in the Tennis Court Garden and Gravel Garden. We plant them deeply, allowing them to escape summer irrigation. Species tulips, such as *Tulipa acuminata*, *T. clusiana*, and *T. linifolia* tend to be long-lived and thrive in the dry soil of the Gravel Garden and Pond Arbor. *Tulipa clusiana* 'Lady Jane' appears rosy-red on cloudy days, but when the sun warms the flowers, they fully open, showing their white interior. The small flowers combine well with other small flowers such as *Narcissus* 'Hawera', with soft yellow blooms, and the spikes of *Muscari armeniacum*, which are blue-purple.

Unlike most tulips that disappear after a year or two, *Tulipa clusiana* 'Lady Jane' reliably returns each year and has a graceful look in the Rock Ledge.

Winter aconites (*Eranthis hyemalis*) and snowdrops (*Galanthus elwe-sii*, *G. nivalis*, and *G. nivalis* 'Flore Pleno') begin the spring bulb season. They may open on sunny midwinter days or be covered by snow well into late winter, opening a day or two after snowmelt. They are dormant by mid-spring, conveniently covered by ferns or other perennials. Both transplant easily in leaf and multiply quickly with division. *Eranthis* spreads easily from seed collected in mid-spring and sown directly where wanted. Seedlings bloom within four to five years. Purchased tubers are usually so desiccated that only a fraction grow. Spring snowflake (*Leucojum vernum*) blooms with snowdrops, but has fused white petals. Rare in the trade, ours were gifts in leaf from friends and thrive in the moist soil near the Ponds alongside later blooming snake's head fritillary (*Fritillaria meleagris*). Our lawn planting of fritillary was inspired by a similar one at Oxford University, England. The fritillaries bloom the same time as summer snowflake (*Leucojum aestivum*), which is taller and easier to buy than its early spring cousin.

Anemone blanda forms low mats 5 to 7 inches tall with large white, pink, or blue flowers much larger than their fernlike leaves. We soak the tubers before planting since they often arrive desiccated. *Anemone*

At its grandest in spring, the Ponds' Silver Bed is a floral dreamscape of bulbs, spring ephemerals, and perennials on a woodland edge.

Snake's head fritillary
(*Fritillaria meleagris*) blooms
in spring near the Pond
Garden.

appenina, the lesser known of the two species in cultivation, has formed large clumps underneath the dogwoods in the Orchard. This Italian native is 8 inches high with light blue flowers held high above the lacy green foliage, an excellent companion for our native wildflowers. Most of our plants have come from seed.

"Tommies" (*Crocus tommasinianus*) have persisted for several decades near the Apple House, because of their rodent resistance and ability to self-sow. Their pale lilac flower color goes well with snowdrops. The larger Dutch crocuses will thrive if rodents have not feasted on them. *Cyclamen coum* and *C. hederifolium* are reliably hardy for us, with good drainage and minimal competition from other plants. Underneath *Magnolia sieboldii* in Minder Woods are long-established clumps of *C. coum* that flower with winter aconites and snowdrops. The heart-shaped leaves are dappled silver and contrast well with the fragrant white to magenta flowers. This cyclamen slowly increases with age and by seeds. *Cyclamen hederifolium* usually flowers when the katsura leaves turn color in autumn. The less hardy *C. purpurascens* survives in a protected microclimate in Minder Woods.

As midspring warms, ornamental onions take on a starring role. The Tennis Court becomes a pointillist landscape, with globes of *Allium hollandicum* 'Purple Sensation', *A. giganteum*, *A.* 'Globemaster', and *A.* 'Gladiator'. *Allium atropurpureum* performs a similar role in the Pond

Seldom used in gardens, *Allium nigrum* has glistening globes of white flowers set with green black ovaries.

Even though *Cyclamen purpurascens* (pictured) is less hardy than *C. coum* or *C. hederifolium*, it thrives unexpectedly in the shade of Minder Woods.

Garden, complemented by the more diminutive blue *A. caeruleum* and the yellow *A. moly*. Onion foliage often looks tattered by the time of bloom, but surrounding perennials hide the unsightly brown. *Allium christophii* has the biggest heads of the alliums, resembling a burst of fireworks. The low plants thrive in the Gravel Garden's full sun, little competition, and excellent drainage. Our native ramps (*A. tricoccum*) send out texturally lined, bluish green leaves in early spring, go dormant in mid-spring May, and then bloom in early summer on naked stalks about 4 inches tall. A single bloom stalk would be lost, but a mass of a hundred is a wonderful sight. We've planted thousands in Bell's Woodland.

Nonhardy bulbs give us blasts of summer color. Mexican native coral drops (*Bessera elegans*), in the Gravel Garden and in seasonal containers, has pendulous red flowers in late summer to early autumn. *Gladiolus murielae*, fragrant and white with a maroon throat, is inexpensive to buy and works well in late-summer plantings. The smaller statured *G.* 'Atom' sports elegant, open-faced flowers of bright red with a perfect

LEFT   Deeply saturated ornamental onion (*Allium hollandicum* 'Purple Sensation') is a signature plant generously used throughout Chanticleer. We top up existing plantings each autumn.

RIGHT   *Nectaroscordum siculum* subsp. *bulgaricum* (formerly *Allium bulgaricum*) has umbels of bell-shaped flowers with interior maroon striations and blooms with early summer perennials.

The 'Karma Corona' dahlia is an outstanding cactus-flowered type with sunset tones of oranges and salmons.

With its distinctive pinwheel burgundy flowers, *Dahlia* 'Verrone's Obsidian' causes notebooks to be scribbled in and cameras to click.

rim of pure white around each petal. It looks marvelous when back-lighted and never fails to impress when the blossoms pop out amongst summer borders.

Several specimens of South African bulbs, *Cyrtanthus* and *Haemanthus,* were grown from seed that Jonathan Wright and Laurel Voran brought back from an inspiration-seeking botanical expedition in 2006. The Eastern Cape of South Africa has warm, moist summers similar to those we experience in our part of Pennsylvania. Many summer bulbs can be easily planted right along with other summer seasonal plants, and they make marvelous highlights when they emerge a bit later. For winter, depending on the bulb, we dig it and store it indoors or, if it's potted, we bring the pot inside.

Dahlias are the signature summer bulbs (technically tubers), carrying the garden until the frosts of autumn. We plant them in full sun and well-drained rich soil. They usually produce two flowering flushes, one in early summer and, following a midsummer lull, in autumn. Cool nights spur prolific flowering, as expected given dahlias' montane origins in Mexico. *Dahlia coccinea* has willowy stems and single orange flowers that fit well in the flowery lawn on the Terraces and in the Winter Shrub Border. Dark-leafed 'Bishop of Llandaff' (red flowers), 'David Howard' (orange), and the Mystic series of dahlias were selected for compact habit and mix well with the perennials of the Tennis Court. 'Verrone's Obsidian' is a staff and visitor favorite for its single blossoms with curled, deep burgundy petals.

One of the best cut flowers in the garden is the spectacular *Dahlia* 'Glorie van Heemstede', a luminously clear yellow water lily type with strong stems. The Karma series of dahlias are excellent for their sturdy stems and longevity in a vase, including 'Fuchsiana' (bright fuchsia with a yellow center), 'Choc' (burgundy black), and 'Corona' (a mix of salmon and yellow). We also cut huge, "dinner-plate" dahlias for arrangements, including 'Emory Paul' (pink flowers), 'Wisconsin Red' (deep red on dark stems), 'Mrs. I. De Ver Warner' (early, rose pink), and 'Thomas Edison' (fuchsia-colored). Older tubers result in larger, robust plants that flower longer.

Most dahlias need staking because of their top-heavy growth and large flowers. Jonathan Wright props them with copper tube hoops, while Emma Seniuk weaves string among the stems, tying them to one bamboo cane. They dig dahlias after frost, leaving some soil clinging to the tubers, and crate them in a potting mix of composted pine bark (peat-based mixes overly dry the tubers). We store the crates of tubers in a cool, dark place until they are brought out for early summer planting. Any precocious leggy shoots are pruned off to encourage subsequent sturdier ones.

Introduced in 1929 and named for the famous inventor with his approval, *Dahlia* 'Thomas Edison' is a strong grower with 6- to 8-inch dark purple flowers.

Bulbs at Chanticleer

ERIC HSU

Bulbs, like tropicals, are essential for the out-sized floral expression that is quintessentially Chanticleer. Generally adaptable and colorful, hardy bulbs feature prominently throughout the garden, concentrating colors in sections. Despite being less easy to place, summer- and autumn-flowering bulbs like lilies, colchicums, and cyclamens extend the exuberance of spring bulbs. There is hardly a part of Chanticleer devoid of bulbs: Even in the largely native Bell's Run, rogue clumps of snowdrops can be found. Our prevailing style of bulb planting is loose and informal, a naturalizing concept that originated with the self-styled Scottish 'Daffodil King' Peter Barr and was promoted in William Robinson's *The Wild Garden* (1870). From early to mid-spring, the Orchard overflows with daffodils sparkling beneath flowering cherries, crabapples, and dogwoods. Chionodoxas, scillas, and Grecian windflowers unify the disparate groups.

In formal areas at Chanticleer House and at the Entrance, bulbs are casually mixed with cool-season annuals and early perennials. Rarely do we resort to solid color blocks, and mixing safeguards the pitfalls of being dependent on a single display easily gone in an unseasonal spring heat wave. This interplanting has the added advantage of concealing dying bulb foliage. *Lunaria annua* 'Variegata' and *Mertensia virginica* loosen the stiff appearance of tulips in the Pond Garden, while in the Cut Flower Garden, aquilegias, woodland forget-me-nots (*Myosotis sylvatica*), and bishop's flower (*Ammi majus*) play off the bulbs. These self-sowing companions have mingled companionably with the strong shapes of tulips as well as those of alliums and Oriental poppies. They have clean, bright colors rivaling the bulbs' saturated hues.

Keeping the bulbs within scale of each other in a mixed planting can be effective, which Joe Henderson has demonstrated in the Silver Bed near the Pond Garden. All the flowers are diminutive and delicate in color and form—the pendulous, soft yellows of *Narcissus* 'Hawera' and the dark blue-purple spikes of grape hyacinth (*Muscari armeniacum*) are classic together, while the tight red lips of *Tulipa clusiana* 'Lady Jane' kick the genteel pastel scheme out of its comfort zone without being overpowering. Replace 'Hawara' with any of the large-flowered daffodils and the result would be out of scale. Even the perennials are proportioned well— *Phlox subulata* and *Erigeron pulchellus* are hardly brash. *Lychnis flos-cuculi* 'Jenny' covers up the dying bulb foliage with its shaggy, soft, lavender-pink blooms. *Narcissus cantabricus*, a species from the southern Mediterranean region, bookends the season in early December with its pure white petticoat flowers. Like other bulbs in this bed, it is relatively small at 4 to 9 inches tall.

Tulipa clusiana 'Lady Jane' has the added benefit of transitioning between the relatively cooler feel of the Silver Bed and the bolder, brighter effect of the Wildflower Slope, where magenta flowers of self-sowing *Lunaria annua* propel upward with the blood-red 'Jan Reus' and 'National Velvet' tulips.

On the other side of the Ponds, Joe Henderson planted snake's head fritillary (*Fritillaria meleagris*), spring snowflake (*Leucojum vernum*), and Siberian squill (*Scilla siberica*). Given the right conditions (moist and cool, weakened turf, and no foot traffic), the snakehead fritillary naturalizes well and varies in color from white to purple. It has self-seeded in the adjoining moss. The flowers, beautifully checkered in rich or dark purple, reward the intrepid visitor who strays off the well-trod path. Although Joe feels that the white-flowered fritillaries stand by themselves and lighten up the darker ones, he has sprinkled in Siberian squill, with its iridescent blue petals, for some color dynamic. On the edges of the area are spring snowflakes, which flower earlier than the fritillaries and appreciate the same damp habitat.

Small is beautiful: *Muscari armeniacum*, *Narcissus* 'Hawera', and *Tulipa clusiana* 'Lady Jane' are in proportion with each other, and *Phlox subulata* offers a horizontal plane from which these bulbs pop.

True lilies are in the genus *Lilium*. Unlike other bulbs, they remain green throughout the growing season, only going dormant for the winter. They add bright splashes of color in early summer, make great cut flowers, and are often fragrant. Most grow in full sun or light shade in well-drained soil. 'Citronella' is tall, with lemon-yellow recurved petals covered in tiny maroon dots. We grow it on the edge of Asian Woods, interspersed with *Syneilesis palmata*. *Lilium lancifolium* is vigorous, reaching 6 feet, with bright orange flowers with recurved petals and maroon dots. It grows on sturdy stems on the edge of Asian Woods. 'Brunello' has strong 4-foot stems and deep orange color. In the Cut Flower Garden, the soft orange *L*. 'Swansea' brightens up what is otherwise a subdued color theme in early summer.

Lilies make a strong summer stand in the Tennis Court Garden. The African Queen strain of lily has 6- to 8-inch-long trumpet-shaped flowers of rich apricot. 'Barcelona' has red-orange, upright-facing flowers on 3-foot stalks. 'Sixth Sense' has fragrant, outward-facing, wine-red flowers edged in white margins. *Lilium pumilum* is shorter, to 2 feet, with fragrant red flowers with reflexed petals. In midsummer, the reflexed, orange petals of tiger lilies (*L. lancifolium*) lead a theme of orange, joined by kniphofias on the ground and *Lantana* 'Zinn Orange' and *Begonia* 'Sparks Will Fly' on the steps. Tiger lilies tower to 8 feet with leaning stems lined with bulbils in the leaf axils, which drop and grow where they land. As the lilies die down in late summer, their declining foliage is concealed by *Calamagrostis ×acutiflora* 'Karl Foerster'.

Orienpet lilies, crosses between Oriental and trumpet lilies, perform well since their flowers are resistant to heat and sun bleaching. The Long Border features the 8-foot-tall 'Scheherazade', which forms secondary and tertiary flower buds that prolong the display. This outstanding lily has 6- to 7-inch-wide light red flowers margined with soft yellow, adding garden color at mid-level. In the Parking Lot Garden, 'Saltarello' offers a rich peach color with bronze anthers.

Martagon lilies have attractive whorls of leaves, nodding flowers with reflexed petals, and grow best in light shade. Dan Benarcik used the Paisley strain of mixed colors near a purple beech tree at the Chanticleer House, and the mixed copper and pink tones of the blooms work splendidly with the newly emerging bronze foliage of the beech and of autumn fern (*Dryopteris erythrosora* 'Brilliance'). Mixed with the nearby hydrangeas, *Lilium* 'Casa Blanca' emits such a strong fragrance in the circle, you would think the hydrangeas were creating it. The 4- to 6-foot stems rise just above the hydrangeas. Our native lilies tend to do best with light shade and are quiet delights with smaller, more subtle flowers. They include *L. superbum*, *L. philadelphicum*, *L. michiganense*, and *L. canadense*. Rarer is *L. grayi*, in the Pond Garden, which is restricted in the wild to North Carolina, Virginia, and Tennessee. Its red-orange flowers are bell-shaped, held high at 4 feet.

Himalayan lily (*Cardiocrinum*) is a lily relative with large white trumpets at the top of the plant; it is not often seen in this area. Having wider leaves than true lilies, it is native to cool mountainous regions, and therefore suffers in our summer heat and winter cold. The narrow, white, trumpet-shaped flowers are fragrant in the evening. Lisa Roper has good success with *C. giganteum* (6 to 7 feet tall), its black-stemmed variety *C. giganteum* var. *yunnanense*, and the shorter *C. cathayanum*, which seeds for us. In early spring, before most perennials have emerged, up come the glossy, red-veined, heart-shaped leaves. Lisa divides the bulbs after they bloom, and the offsets flower within four years.

LEFT   Few lilies are as robust and prolific as tiger lilies (*Lilium lancifolium*). Over the years, they have formed impressive colonies in the Tennis Court Garden.

RIGHT   Himalayan lily (*Cardiocrinum cathayanum*) may be shorter in stature than its taller cousins *C. giganteum* and *C. giganteum* var. *yunnanense*, but it has similar trumpet-shaped white flowers marked with red stripes, and it self-seeds in Asian Woods.

The Orchard Bulb Lawn

Lisa Roper recalls her design and its inception for the Orchard bulb planting: "We planted 40,000 bulbs in the fall of 1991. In subsequent years, we brought the number up to 100,000. Chris Woods dreamed up the idea and gave me the job of picking the bulbs and drawing up the plan for a "river of bulbs" in the Orchard. The idea was to use narcissus with pale colors, avoiding all-yellow cultivars, to prevent clashing with the strong flower color of some of the crabapples. We picked daffodil cultivars that were strong growers to compete with the turf, and we wanted early and late-season bloomers for a sequence of flowering."

Narcissus 'Ice Follies' opens the display in early spring with a pale yellow cup and white petals. *Narcissus* 'Bravoure' follows—white with a long, bright yellow trumpet. These early daffodils bloom with the pink 'Accolade' cherry. *Narcissus* 'Salome', with a small, apricot-yellow flower, blooms with the yellow *Magnolia* 'Elizabeth'. *Narcissus* 'Actaea' and 'Ice Wings' finish the season, flowering in mid-spring. For even earlier bloom, we could have used *N.* 'February Gold', 'February Silver', 'Peeping Tom', and 'Tête-à-Tête'. They bloom in late winter in the Gravel Garden and in the Winter Shrub Border. *Narcissus* 'Jet Fire' is an early, short daffodil with yellow petals and orange cup that blooms outside the Ruin.

Layers of blue scillas, chionodoxas, ipheions, and grape hyacinths complement the daffodils. Scillas and chionodoxas seed about and form larger colonies in sun and shade. Growing together, they create a subtle mix of colors. The colder blue of the downward-facing scillas strengthens the warmer, purple-blue of the upward-facing chionodoxas. To distinguish them fully, look at the petals: chionodoxa's petals are fused whereas scilla's are separate. *Scilla siberica* 'Spring Beauty' has larger flowers and sturdier stems than the species. *Chionodoxa forbesii* 'Blue Giant' has lavender-blue flowers with a white eye, and *C. sardensis* has smaller, dark blue flowers and no white eye.

Grape hyacinth (*Muscari armeniacum*) naturalizes well in part shade where the grass is not so impenetrable. Foliage of *M. armeniacum* emerges in the early autumn and persists through the winter. Its foliage should not be mown, since it is photosynthesizing. *Muscari botryoides* has similar blue flowers but flushes new foliage in late winter. Its fresh leaves look better in the spring than those of the more common *M. armeniacum*. Spring starflower (*Ipheion uniflorum*) is rarely seen in gardens; it naturalizes in well-drained soil in sun or part shade, increasing with offsets and seeds. Flowering in midspring, after the scillas and chionodoxas, the bluish star-shaped flowers smell like citrus blossoms and the leaves like onion. *Ipheion* 'Rolf Fiedler' and 'Wisley Blue' are deeper blue.

TOP   The intense spring leaves of *Acer palmatum* 'Bloodgood' pick up the red-orange cups of *Narcissus* 'Barrett Browning' in the Orchard Bulb Lawn.

BOTTOM   Grape hyacinth (*Muscari armeniacum*) naturalizes in partial shade. The muscari's autumn foliage is a disadvantage because it often looks tattered by bloom time.

Pale-hued daffodils, like *Narcissus* 'Barrett Browning', are easier to use with other colors, whereas strong yellows are more likely to clash with crabapples and other spring-bloomers.

The Bulb Meadow

We have planted several lawn areas with bulbs, giving a meadow effect. One area has been named the Bulb Meadow and is above Asian Woods. It began as a planting of colchicums in the hillside lawn. These mauve-flowered bulbs bloom in early autumn without their hostalike leaves, which appear in late winter and go dormant in early summer. This lawn planting was inspired by a similar hillside at Winterthur in Delaware, which was probably inspired by a planting in England. Since the area is not mowed in the spring because of the bulb leaves, we added spring- and summer-blooming bulbs as well. The Bulb Meadow has become an excellent study of longevity and succession of bloom.

First to bloom is *Hyacinthus orientalis* 'Blue Festival', a fragrant blue with a more relaxed look than the more common cultivars of hyacinth. Next come small-flowered daffodils, chosen for their grace and soft colors, fitting the naturalistic feel of the meadow—*Narcissus* 'Elka' (diminutive, creamy white flowers) and 'Hawera' (grasslike foliage and small, bell-cupped yellow flowers). Spanish bluebells (*Hyacinthoides hispanica*) are next; they have seeded on the hillside. In late spring, *Camassia leichtlinii* 'Semiplena' blooms creamy white, the last of the spring-bloomers.

We mow the grass and the matured bulb foliage in early summer. In midsummer, surprise lily (*Lycoris squamigera*) sends up 3-foot shoots of pink trumpets without their leaves, blooming for a month. We try to mow the grass at least once when they finish. The low grass sets the stage for colchicums, often called autumn crocus (which is actually a different bulb), flowering for the rest of early to mid-autumn. Performing best are the large-flowered, vigorous *Colchicum* 'Lilac Wonder' and 'The Giant' ('The Giant' has a white throat). We also include in the mix *C. byzantinum*, *C. speciosum*, and the cultivars 'Violet Queen' and 'Waterlily'. Neither deer nor rodents eat the poisonous, long-lived colchicums, which become more impressive each year.

The Creek Garden is also a spring bulb meadow. Lining Bell's Run are over 20,000 *Camassia leichtlinii* subsp. *suksdorfii* 'Blauwe Donau', accentuating the curves of the stone-lined creek. The deep blue camassias bloom in mid-spring and tolerate flooding. Planted in the lawn, we let the camassia foliage mature, and then we mow as summer begins.

TOP Preceding the colchicums, surprise lily (*Lycoris squamigera*) is sometimes called naked lily because the flowers appear without leaves in midsummer.

BOTTOM Bulb plantings are strongest with large concentrations of bulbs. We've planted thousands of colchicums in the Bulb Meadow, producing an impressive display in early autumn.

Sweeps of *Camassia leichtlinii* subsp. *suksdorfii* 'Blauwe Donau' relish the moist verges of the creek at Bell's Run.

Annual Grasses with Bulbs and Other Plantings

Inspired by the beauty of grains in the Serpentine, Jonathan Wright uses annual grasses with spring plants. Rye and wheat seedlings cover the soil, eliminating muddy backdrops and splashes to the bulbs, and give a soft, meadow-like effect to the planting. He has broadcast winter rye in autumn, after planting tulips, narcissus, and crocus, raking the seeds into the top inch of soil. The rye grows in the cool fall weather and overwinters well. Similar results were achieved by sowing wheat in late winter, doubling the seeds for quicker fill. He has also used annual grasses for sculptural effect, such as planting a circle of winter rye and yellow tulips, surrounded by purple tulips. The rye "hedges" reinforce the circular pattern of the yellow tulips. After the bulbs bloom, he lifts them with garden forks, and incorporates the rye grass into the soil as green manure. With perennial bulb plantings, we cut the rye and wheat just before they set seed so they don't become weedy.

Emma Seniuk uses bunnytail grass (*Lagurus ovatus*) in a similar way in the Cut Flower Garden. She starts the seed in flats in the winter and grows this cool-season annual grass in cold frames. She plants them out in mid-spring, using some in masses and some woven throughout the entire area. The large, fluffy seed heads on the 20-inch-tall plants combine and complement the other spring plantings and they cut well for arrangements.

Winter rye broadcast in late winter gives a semblance of a flowery meadow in the Teacup Garden.

Bunnytail grass (*Lagarus ovatus*) is an annual, cool-season grass that fills in around spring bulbs and keeps the display attractive before and after the bulbs bloom.

PERENNIALS, ANNUALS, AND GRASSES

Perennials, annuals, and grasses are all herbaceous plants, meaning they die to the ground in the winter. Their counterpart in the garden is the woody plants, the trees and shrubs. Herbaceous plants have great use in the garden because they grow quickly, providing rapid change in one growing year. An herbaceous planting, such as in the Pond Garden, begins spring as an almost flat plane, with long views and an open feeling. By summer, the area is more enclosed, with plants of various heights, and by late summer, the area is almost secretive.

Shade

Shade is as variable as the moisture conditions in any given spot. We have wet shade as well as dry, very deep shade on the north sides of buildings, and dappled shade under tall trees. Our shady areas include Asian Woods, Bell's Woodland, the Wildflower Slope, and Minder Woods. Foliage is key in shade designs, since plants don't bloom as heavily in the shade. Spring ephemerals provide a burst of color under trees before the leaves fill in, and some plants, such as hydrangeas and hostas, bloom well in the shade.

Foliage for Shade

You could plant a beautiful shade garden simply using hostas, ferns, and epimediums. These tough plants are textural and colorful, as demonstrated in Asian Woods. They can be multiplied by division, so it can be relatively inexpensive to have an impressive display.

Hostas have attractive leaves and flowers. *Hosta* 'Emerald Tiara' is low growing and golden, quickly spreading to fill a space. It shines under a holly near the Entrance and in Asian Woods. 'Blue Angel' is the largest hosta in Asian Woods, with bluish leaves and standing 3 feet tall. Other big-leaved hostas include 'Frances Williams', 'Krossa Regal', 'Royal Standard', and 'Sum and Substance'. 'Sagae' is a large plant used throughout Asian Woods for its striking variegation, a frosty gray-green leaf with creamy yellow margins. Among the best hostas for flowers are *H. plantaginea* and its offspring 'Royal Standard' (both with white, fragrant flowers against green leaves in Minder Woods), *H. yingeri* (a small plant with lavender flowers in Asian Woods), and the diminutive *H. tardiflora*, blooming last, with small lavender flowers. *Hosta yingeri* is named for Barry Yinger, a plant explorer who has specialized in Asian plants. Barry documented the species in southwestern South Korea in 1985.

For textural contrast, pair large-leaved *Hosta tokudama*, with its puckered, cupped, glaucous leaves, with hakone grass (*Hakonechloa macra* 'Aureola'), a low-shade grass with variegated yellow and green foliage. *Hakonechloa* brightens the shaded area, and the almost rounded, blue

Large, tiered mounds of *Hosta* 'Blue Angel' spill over the bamboo fences underneath sycamore trees in Asian Woods.

leaves of the hosta complement in color and form. Such contrasting foliage textures and colors make strong visual statements that last many months.

Epimediums thrive under the mature trees of Asian Woods, requiring little care other than cutting to the ground in late winter. *Epimedium* 'Amber Queen' has large, holly-shaped leaves with orange flowers. The earliest epimedium to bloom is *E. stellulatum*. Ours is a long-leafed form, given to us by Richard Lighty, former director of Delaware's Mt. Cuba Center. A froth of pure white flowers on black stems rises above the spiny, elongated leaves. Several other Chinese epimediums come from Massachusetts plant explorer and breeder Darrell Probst. His introduction of *E. wushanense* stands 2½ feet tall with thick, narrow 8-inch leaflets. Pale yellow flowers hang like tiny wisteria clusters. These epimediums are clumpers rather than spreaders, and we use them as focal points rather than ground covers. On the other hand, spreading *E. ×versicolor* 'Sulphureum' and *E. ×warleyense* 'Orangekönigin' form thick, indestructible masses of heart-shaped leaves, emerging flushed with red, followed by yellow and orange flowers, respectively, held on wiry stems.

Upside-down fern, *Arachniodes standishii*, has large, graceful fronds that appear flipped over. Under them in Asian Woods flows a low, dark stream of black mondo grass (*Ophiopogon planiscapus* 'Nigrescens').

Hakone grass (*Hakonechloa macra*) is a green study of restrained elegance. It is less common than its variegated selection 'Aureola'.

OPPOSITE Gold rivulets of *Hosta* 'Emerald Tiara' flow around larger *H.* 'Fortunei Aureomarginata' in Asian Woods. The hostas conceal the bare spaces vacated by pink primrose (*Primula sieboldii*) during summer dormancy.

Flushed red at their edges, young spring leaves of *Epimedium* ×*versicolor* 'Sulphureum' are illuminated like stained glass. Short-spurred pale yellow flowers appear ahead of the leaves.

The fern and the ophiopogon remain dramatic from spring through autumn. Chinese mayapple, *Podophyllum pleianthum*, does not go dormant in late summer like our native *P. peltatum*. Growing up to 2 feet tall, its umbrella-shaped, glossy leaves hide burgundy flowers underneath (foul-smelling and pollinated by flies). *Podophyllum* 'Spotty Dotty' has large, attractive leaves with purple blotches. *Paris polyphylla* is a challenge to grow, but thrives at the foot of a rough stone wall in a cool, moist, shaded area in the Creek Garden. *Primula veris* thrives alongside with a burst of lemon yellow in the early spring. *Syneilesis aconitifolia* and *S. palmata* have a textural effect similar to *Paris*, but thrive in dry shade.

The sweetshrubs *Calycanthus chinensis* and *C.* ×*raulstonii* 'Hartlage Wine' are large plants, 8 to 10 feet tall. Red-flowered 'Hartlage Wine' blooms profusely every summer under the dry shade of sycamores and red maple. For weeks in late spring, its branches are laden with large, burgundy-red flowers. Unfortunately, neither plant has fragrance, unlike our native Carolina allspice (*C. floridus*). Evergreen aucubas thrive in dry shade under pines in Asian and Minder Woods. *Aucuba japonica* 'Picturata' has a large golden splash in the middle of each leaf with golden speckles against the green outer edges; 'Variegata' has golden speckled leaves. Both are females, producing large, red, oblong berries. A subtler choice is *A. japonica* 'Salicifolia', also a female, with long, narrow, shiny green leaves. Aucubas need protection from winter winds and sun, so they are perfect beneath evergreens.

LEFT   Upside-down fern (*Arachniodes standishii*) has gone through multiple name changes, and was formerly placed in the genera *Dryopteris* and *Polystichum*.

RIGHT   The yellow splotches of *Aucuba japonica* 'Variegata' appear to be the work of an artist going drip-crazy with a paintbrush. The splotches especially jump out when the red berries are ripe. This Japanese denizen tolerates deep, dry shade in Minder Woods.

Joe Loves *Paris*

JOE HENDERSON

I finally found a perfect place for growing *Paris polyphylla*, a plant I coveted after seeing it in England. I grow it at the foot of a rough stone wall in a cool and moist area shaded by cryptomerias alongside the astilbe bed beside Bell's Run. I am now trying to find suitable mates to grow alongside the *Paris* without outcompeting it. *Primula veris* grows nearby, but a primula somehow doesn't seem a suitable pairing. Perhaps something more woodsy, like a small fern or a clubmoss like *Selaginella kraussiana*. I like the simple clubmoss pairing, with contrasting texture and the dark green of the *Paris* against the lighter yellow green of the selaginella.

Rare in cultivation and particular about its growth requirements, *Paris polyphylla* has showy red fruits like a ruby brooch. Joe grows this *Trillium* relative from China in cool, moist, acidic soil and light shade.

Dry Shade

LISA ROPER

Deep shade under a surface-rooted tree is a tough spot to grow anything. The tree roots suck most of the moisture, leaving little for any underplantings. Some wonderful shade perennials accommodate these conditions, but they may need help getting established. I incorporate organic soil amendments and do regular watering until the plants have rooted. Directly sowing seeds also helps. Once established, they will tolerate the dry conditions.

Japanese sacred lily (*Rohdea japonica*) is a clump-forming perennial with dark green, strap-like, evergreen leaves about 1 foot long. Planted in mass at the base of European hornbeam, they resemble a sweep of narrow-leaved hostas. Low in the foliage, short stalks hold fat red berries that persist through winter. I increased the numbers of rohdea by propagating by seed. I picked ripe fruits, removed the fleshy coating, washed the seeds, and planted them ½ inch deep in a pot with potting soil. I stored the pot in a cold frame (a refrigerator would work) for two months before setting it in a greenhouse (or windowsill) to germinate. I kept the soil moist during the storage period, but very little watering was needed because of the cool temperatures.

Since texture and form are almost more important than flowers when it comes to shade plants, another favorite of mine for dry spots is *Boehmeria spicata*, a benign relative of stinging nettle. This bold-leafed perennial, with opposite, rounded leaves, grows under a red maple. The edges of the leaves look like they have been cut with pinking shears. *Boehmeria* flowers in summer with upright spikes of tiny white flowers, but the curious leaves and the obvious contrast to the finer textured plants really set it apart. Pair it with a fine-textured *Carex conica* 'Snowline' or the delicate foliage of dwarf aruncus.

A nonstinging member of the nettle family (Urticaceae), *Boehmeria spicata* was once harvested for its fibers and woven into cloth in Japan. In Asian Woods, its prominent leaf tips for shedding excess water offer a decorative role.

Flowers for Shade

On the Wildflower Slope and in Bell's Woodland, the blue and white cultivars of native *Phlox divaricata* and *P. stolonifera* brighten the shade in the spring. They are easily multiplied by division and cuttings. Joe Henderson plants light-colored flowers predominantly in the deep shade and darker flowers in more sunlight. In the Creek Garden, he overplanted them with sweet-smelling *Rhododendron austrinum*.

For bragging rights, nothing impresses like orchids, but not all hardy, terrestrial orchids are difficult to grow. Chinese ground orchid (*Bletilla striata*) and several species of terrestrial orchid (*Calanthe*) send up showy spikes of flowers in early spring to early summer in Asian Woods. Rich, moist soil and light shade seem best for them. Lisa Roper has had amazing success with Japanese ladyslipper (*Cypripedium japonicum*) in Asian Woods. Its pair of leaves resembles a ballerina skirt flaring out, with the dainty, lavender ladyslipper flowers rising above. It blooms for over three weeks. The plant is expensive and rare in nurseries. Lisa successfully divides the plants in the spring as they emerge. You'll find its American cousins *C. parviflorum* (yellow) on the Wildflower Slope, and *C. reginae* (pink) reigns in the Bog next to the Ponds. Spiraling in front of it are the dainty white, late-summer flowers of *Spiranthes odorata*. It is best cultivated in moist semishade but, once established, will colonize areas that are less than ideal—even dry sunny spots.

LEFT   One of the early flowering terrestrial orchids that demands woodland conditions, *Calanthe tricarinata* has green-yellow tepals with frilled red lips marked with white.

RIGHT   At summer's finale, *Anemone ×hybrida* 'Whirlwind' has a cool presence, with its semidouble 2-inch white flowers on tall stems with jagged green leaves.

A terrestrial orchid widespread in Japan but expensive and rare in cultivation in America, *Cypripedium japonicum* has formed healthy colonies in Asian Woods. Its single pink ladyslipper flower emerges from a pair of pleated leaves like an unfolding Japanese fan.

A delightful, self-sowing shade dweller, *Impatiens balfourii* is a pizzazz of bright color in shady nooks of Asian Woods.

A few shade plants are notable for their autumnal blooms. Leopard plant (*Ligularia fischeri*) stands like a torch in Asian Woods with bright yellow, sweetly fragrant flowers. Lisa Roper originally got this plant as a division. It didn't bloom the first four years and then threw a short, single bloom in the fifth autumn. The following spring, she divided the plant and spread it along the path in more sunlight. The clumps thrived and grew to three times the size, flowering at 6 feet tall and becoming a prominent late-season feature in the woods.

Lower in stature and more subtle, American natives coral bells (*Heuchera villosa*) and white wood aster (*Eurybia divaricata*) bloom in late summer and early autumn along the base of the arbor in the Gravel Garden and in Bell's Woodland. *Tricyrtis* and *Anemone japonica* (and its cousins) are indispensable in Asian and Minder Woods for livening up an otherwise quiet time. Easily divided, they quickly fill holes for late summer display.

Self-seeders, including late spring–blooming *Hesperis matronalis* and summer-flowering *Impatiens balfourii* and *I. capensis*, add extra color to shady areas. All of these seed prolifically in the shade, but are easily pulled where you don't want them. Hesperis has naturalized along our country roads. Throughout the summer and fall, the bushy plants of *Impatiens balfourii* are covered in small pink and white orchidlike flowers. Some call it touch-me-not, because ripened seed pods send seed flying in all directions when touched. *Impatiens capensis* is its native cousin, growing much taller (to 5 feet) with orange flowers.

Fruit Display in Shade

Autumn is a time for fruit display, which can be just as showy as blooms and lasts longer. *Paeonia obovata* and *P. japonica* are woodland peonies boasting blue and red seeds. The seed displays glisten like jewels for a month, whereas their flowers (*P. obovata*, pale pink; *P. japonica*, white) last but a week in the spring. Jack-in-the-pulpit (*Arisaema triphyllum*) is known for its interesting flowers, but in late summer after the leaves die down, its stalks of clustered red fruits shine. Less well known is another American native, *A. dracontium*, with multiple leaflets spreading out like fingers and a flower topped with a narrow, green, hooded cylinder and a long, upward-pointing tongue. It, too, has a cluster of red fruits later in the season. Several of its Asian cousins grow in Asian Woods and put on quite a show: *Arisaema sikokianum* has a prominently colored flower, with the "jack" a bright white and the "pulpit" burgundy; *A. ringens* is shorter, stockier, but makes a big presence with large, tropical-looking glossy leaves. The dark purple and green flowers resemble a cobra tucked under the foliage. It is a robust grower, divides easily, and has red fruits in fall.

LEFT   Nearly hidden by large shiny trifoliate leaves, the cobralike flowers of cobra lily (*Arisaema ringens*) look ready to strike at the unsuspecting visitor.

RIGHT   Blooming for only a week, shade-loving *Paeonia obovata* has a delicate beauty befitting the understated atmosphere of Asian Woods.

Ephemeral Bloom in the Shade

Ephemerals take advantage of spring sunshine and moisture before trees leaf out. They bloom, build up reserves of food, produce seeds, and go dormant, usually before midsummer. The earliest flower in our native areas is skunk cabbage, *Symplocarpus foetidus*. Rub the leaves to understand the common name. It grows best in constantly wet areas, as do its cousins *Lysichiton americanus*, a yellow-flowered West Coast native, and the white-flowered Asian *L. camtschatcensis*. *Symplocarpus* starts blooming in midwinter, but the purple-brown flowers are not showy. Their giant leaves emerge in spring and make a strong statement, but vanish by late summer. *Lysichiton* blooms in spring, with showier, fragrant flowers and big, bold leaves.

Native ephemerals brighten spring. Virginia bluebell (*Mertensia virginica*) opens in early spring, closely followed by the small but cheerful Virginia spring beauty (*Claytonia virginiana*) and then trilliums, the rock stars of the wildflower world. We grow about twenty taxa of *Trillium*, primarily on the Wildflower Slope and in Bell's Woodland. Blooming in mid-spring, they demonstrate their name with three leaves, petals, and sepals. *Trillium sessile* has flowers the color of dried blood, contrasting beautifully with the delicate-looking pure white flowers of false rue anemone (*Enemion biternatum*).

The pristine white blooms of *Trillium grandiflorum* are one of the floral marvels in eastern North American woodlands. Nursery-propagated *Trillium grandiflorum* is easier than other species to establish in the garden. Its white flowers echo the bark on a paper birch's root flare on the Wildflower Slope, and a mass of them fill the path circle in Bell's Woodland. The large flowers gradually fade from white to pink, seeds ripen, and the plant disappears in early summer (a good time to divide them). The low-growing *Carex eburnea* gently grows around trillium crowns, providing a lime green for the rest of the summer. Cardinal flower (*Lobelia cardinalis*) and Indian pink (*Spigelia marilandica*) bloom red in the summer and keep a flow of color going. Both are easily grown by casting ripe seed on the ground where you want the plants to grow, no digging needed. Avalanche lily (*Erythronium* 'Pagoda') finishes the ephemeral show with large yellow nodding flowers. It is a brassy hybrid of our native fawn lilies, *E. revolutum* and *E. tuolumnense*.

Once ephemerals go dormant, you need to deal with the empty space right away while you can still remember where it is so you do not accidentally damage them. Late-emerging perennials are a good match. The yellow flowers of ephemeral *Adonis amurensis* 'Fukujukai' open in late winter as the snow melts. Its fernlike foliage frames the flowers, and after bloom, expands into a lacy mound until going dormant in late spring. Japanese toad lily (*Tricyrtis hirta* 'Variegata') starts strong growth about that time. Its speckled, orchidlike blooms appear in autumn on graceful, arching stems. The timing is perfect—a seamless changing of the guard, in the same piece of ground.

Each individual carpel of *Paeonia obovata* splits to reveal metallic blue fertile seeds embedded among scarlet infertile ones.

Indian pink (*Spigelia marilandica*), once used by Native Americans for ceremonial purposes, has striking red tubular flowers with yellow throats that recall a court jester's cap or a firecracker. Like *Trillium grandiflorum*, it is threatened by overcollecting.

TOP   In mid-spring, *Trillium grandiflorum* forms a sheet of white flowers in the informally named trillium circle. It has taken Przemek Walczak a few years to achieve this effect, and now the clumps are multiplying and self-seeding.

BOTTOM   In the same spot two months later, *Trillium grandiflorum* is dormant, and Indian pink (*Spigelia marilandica*) is the star attraction, luring butterflies and hummingbirds. Most of the *S. marilandica* plants started as small plugs to minimize inadvertent disturbance of the dormant trilliums during planting.

Sun Perennials, Annuals, and Biennials

Sunshine makes for brilliantly colored leaves and flowers. It allows for the exuberance of the Pond Garden, expressed in a hillside of red poppies and orange globeflowers, and with pond-side plantings of the indigo of Japanese irises, a warm cerise of the 'Mrs. Perry D. Slocum' lotus, and the bright candelabra primroses.

There are many annuals and perennials for sunny areas. Perennials provide continuity from year to year and can become old friends in the garden. They bloom for a set period of time, from several weeks to perhaps six weeks. To have continuous bloom in a perennial planting, you need to carefully choose the perennials for a sequence. Annuals give us a blast of color and are quick performers, and they fill voids left in the garden as bulbs pass and early flowering perennials fade. Biennials germinate in summer or fall, blooming the following year and then dying. Many bloom after spring bulbs and before summer perennials.

A Sequence of Color

Flowers can be thought of as bit players at Chanticleer. When you visit on any one day, you see flowers, but you also see the texture and color of foliage. When you return, the constant is the foliage. The flowers are ever changing, adding dynamism to the plantings, but are not here for the long run throughout the season. We've planted for a sequence of bloom from spring through autumn. Bulbs and ephemerals begin the color as spring warms the garden. Mid-spring blossoms of *Allium, Aquilegia, Lupinus, Silene, Campanula, Papaver rhoeas, Salvia nemorosa* 'Caradonna', and *Nepeta* create a tapestry in the Pond Garden. Mediterranean native *Gladiolus communis* subsp. *byzantinus* 'Cruentus' emerges amidst self-sowing *Nassella tenuissima* and woody lavenders in the Gravel Garden, both of which will be showy later. *Paeonia* 'Cytherea' glows in the late afternoon light in the Cut Flower Garden. *Kniphofia* 'Flamenco Mix' and *Salvia nemorosa* 'Caradonna' flow through the Winter Shrub Border, visually uniting with *Iris* 'Cinnabar Red' and *Allium* 'Ambassador' in the Pond Garden.

As we move into late spring, the Rock Ledge above the Pond Garden becomes more yellow and purple with *Ratibida pinnata* and *Echinacea purpurea*. *Aquilegia chrysantha* 'Denver Gold' glitters with the regal purples of *Campanula medium* in the Cut Flower Garden, alongside the white umbels and ferny foliage of *Ammi majus* and *A. visnaga*. *Asclepias tuberosa* flows orange through the Gravel Garden, accenting masses of purple *Thymus, Callirhoe involucrata*, and fragrant *Lavandula*.

Late spring/early summer is a spiky time in the garden. These strong points are emphasized through repetition from the Winter Shrub Border sweeping to the Rock Ledge to the Ponds themselves. Orange spikes of *Kniphofia* punctuate the border, *Verbascum* and *Eremurus* thrust above the Rock Ledge, with *Penstemon digitalis, Digitalis*, and

Gladiolus communis subsp. *byzantinus* 'Cruentus' overwinters for us and produces fantastical white-throated, magenta flowers in mid-spring. Their flowering coincides with *Allium hollandicum* 'Purple Sensation' in the Gravel Garden.

Thermopsis taking up the points in the Pond Garden. The impressively tall foxtail lilies (*Eremurus*) are native to the steppe regions of Afghanistan and central Asia, require well-drained soil, and are intolerant of irrigation. Their roots are fleshy and it is difficult to find fresh, not dried out, roots perhaps because most are imported. We order extras to make up for losses after transplanting.

As summer begins, the sun is directly overhead, making it difficult to photograph in the harsh light except in the early morning and late afternoon. Flowers need to be strong in color to shine. Annual *Monarda citriodora* blooms in the Long Border. *Eutrochium maculatum* 'Gateway' and *Heliopsis helianthoides* 'Summer Nights' bloom in the Cut Flower Garden, with asparagus foliage behind. *Agastache rupestris*, with its welcome fragrant foliage, blooms in the Gravel Garden with spiky *Yucca rostrata* in the background.

Brightening the heat and humidity of midsummer, lotuses bloom in the Ponds, and tall yellow flowers of *Silphium terebinthinaceum* rise up behind the large leaves of *Napaea dioica*. *Lobelia cardinalis*, *Hemerocallis*,

Two different color approaches: The Cut Flower Garden (left) has a precise, controlled grasp of colors, namely yellows and purples: bright yellow smudges of *Isatis tinctoria* enliven the washes of amethyst *Allium hollandicum* 'Purple Sensation', lilac *Hesperis matronalis*, and purple *Iris sibirica* under grapevine-covered rebar arches lending height to the area. In contrast, the Pond Garden's Rock Ledge (right) is freer, more expressive, and less concerned about color clashes: the red *Papaver rhoeas* bleed into white *Penstemon digitalis* 'Husker Red', yellow *Thermopsis caroliniana*, and orange *Kniphofia*.

Full sun areas produce the most blossoms. For example, the blue *Nigella damascena* 'Miss Jekyll' and bright pink *Silene armeria* bloom together in the Rock Ledge.

The dark calyces of *Salvia nemorosa* 'Caradonna' not only offset the flowers well but also prolong the show.

and grasses are ablaze, while *Rudbeckia subtomentosa* 'Henry Eilers' and *Foeniculum vulgare* 'Purpureum' mingle on the Chanticleer Terraces. *Rudbeckia* 'Herbstsonne' is a star of late summer, with its tall stature and two months of bloom followed by persistent seed heads. Blooming with it are *Helianthus ×multiflorus* 'Capenoch Star', *H.* 'Gold Lace', *H. maximiliani* 'Santa Fe', *Tithonia rotundifolia*, *Coreopsis tripteris* 'Lightning Flash', and red *Amaranthus hypochondriacus*.

By early autumn, the angle of the sun is noticeably lower and backlights flowers and foliage. *Platycodon grandiflorus* 'Astra Double Blue' charms near the entrance, and *Helianthus angustifolius* visually explodes along the creek. *Calamagrostis ×acutiflora* 'Karl Foerster', *Helianthus angustifolius* 'First Light', and *Baccharis halimifolia* create an autumn palate in the Pond Garden. *Aster tataricus*, towering to 8 feet tall, and *Pennisetum orientale* at its base, frames a view of the Vegetable Garden archway. *Symphyotrichum oblongifolium* 'October Skies', *Lavandula* foliage and ornamental grasses catch the last of the evening light in the Gravel Garden. A flood of little bluestem follows the path near the Serpentine. *Muhlenbergia capillaris* is a sparkling pink grass on the hill above the Pond Garden; it never fails to impress. *Aconitum carmichaelii* 'Barker's Variety' has intensely blue, pearlescent, hooded flowers along the path near the Pond Garden.

Flowers for Cutting

The Cut Flower Garden is a long, flat rectangle that can be seen in one glance. Since the area must look as good as the flowers do in a vase, all color combinations need to be aesthetically harmonious. The central path, running 120 feet long and 6 feet wide, envelopes guests with overflowing flowers. Arches lend height, as do tall perennials in the center of the beds.

Early spring relies on bulbs, and Emma Seniuk tries new tulip cultivars each year. *Tulipa* 'Negrita', 'Rem's Favourite', and 'Apeldoorn' have perennialized for us. When cut in bud, tulips bloom for a week and bend gracefully toward the light in the vase. Emma groups tulips in blocks that visually drift across the beds, creating continuity through color and form with only three to four cultivars. Bamboo canes delineate the sections as she plants, a trick learned at England's Great Dixter. She applies the same marking method to designate "pockets" of annuals repetitively occurring along the paths. Cool-season annuals include *Calendula officinalis* 'Radio' and *Centaurea cyanus* 'Black Ball' and 'Blue Boy'. She sows the centaureas in autumn. They overwinter in the cold frames prior to spring planting and bloom through early summer if deadheaded.

Lisa Roper likes the bold, round, purple starbursts of alliums in her arrangements. Later in the season, she relies on sunflowers, such as *Helianthus annuus* 'Prado Red', a multiflowering deep red. The strong, long stems of zinnias, such as 'Orange King' (soft orange), 'Canary

CLOCKWISE FROM TOP LEFT   Fall and winter sowings of *Ammi visnaga* (pictured here) result in larger, longer flowering plants than those from spring sowings. *Ammi visnaga* and *A. majus* are excellent fillers in floral arrangements.

Spires of *Verbascum olympicum* become punctuation points towering over the sea of *Papaver rhoeas*, *Salvia nemorosa* 'Caradonna', and *Silene armeria*. The seed heads are left to nourish gold finches and to secure the next generation of self-sown seedlings for the Rock Ledge.

Hot and cold: *Perovskia atriplicifolia* is a cool silvery purple contrast for the red biennial *Ipomopsis rubra* and orange annual *Cosmos sulphureus* in the Winter Shrub Border.

A florist's dream, the Cut Flower Garden is a classic promenade through vine-clad arches and flowery beds.

Watering

While we'd like to have a garden that needs no supplemental water, that simply is not possible, given the types of gardening we do in our region of hot summers. We use plants that will grow well where planted without supplemental water, but in dry periods, we have to irrigate. New plants, of course, need extra water until established. The Gravel Garden is designed to need no watering, as is the low-maintenance Parking Lot Garden. We water our containers by hand with hoses and, when possible, using collected rainwater from our cisterns. Hand-watering allows us to reach only the plants that specifically need it. We water Asian Woods with overhead sprinklers attached to hoses. We try to do this simple way of watering early in the morning or overnight so we lose less to evaporation. Most of our lawns are not irrigated, but the lawns at the Chanticleer Terraces have an in-ground irrigation system.

We avoid overhead watering in the Cut Flower Garden because it can damage flowers and they will not last as long. We water low and away from open flowers. The area does not have good air circulation, so overhead watering can also cause fungal issues, especially on zinnias (and on squashes in the Vegetable Garden). Instead, we water by hand with a hose and watering wand during dry periods. We haven't installed drip irrigation in the Cut Flower Garden because we change the plantings so often.

Bird' (yellow), and 'Oriole' (deep orange) create bouquets of lively summer color.

Long-blooming summer annuals, easily grown from seed or cuttings, satisfy the constant demand for cut flowers. Repetition of *Verbena bonariensis*, with its wiry branching topped with little purple flowers, creates a rhythmic effect throughout the garden. Gomphrenas are good fresh or dried. *Gomphrena* 'Fireworks' has long, jointed stems with pale purple flower heads; *G. haageana* 'Strawberry Fields' has a lower habit and luminous red flowers with yellow accents. *Celosia argentea* var. *cristata* 'Cramer's Lemon Lime' grabs attention with its crested, "brain type," yellow-green flowers.

Although the flowering period for most perennials is only several weeks, perennials are an integral component of the Cut Flower Garden. Herbaceous peonies are glorious and are expensive in the florist shop. The fluorescent pink *Paeonia* 'Cytherea' can be seen from a distance in the garden and livens up our arrangements. Yarrows cut well and bridge the gap between spring and summer. *Achillea filipendulina* 'Parker's Variety' is a favorite for its tall, strong stems culminating in bright yellow flowers.

The long, hot days of summer foster a proliferation of composites. *Rudbeckia subtomentosa* 'Henry Eilers' creates clouds of yellow fluted petals. Unlike other composites that have flat petals, its petals

are rolled, giving a tubular effect. The multistemmed inflorescences become dense arrangements with no need for filler. *Rudbeckia* 'Herbstsonne' has long-lasting flowers on strong stems needing no staking, clean foliage, and it blooms valiantly in the summer heat. Later, *Helianthus maximiliani* 'Santa Fe' towers over the asparagus hedge with bright yellow flowers. For fall arrangements, asters offer a wealth of color options. *Symphyotrichum laeve* 'Bluebird' comes into glory on the Long Border as the summer perennials begin to fade. *Symphyotrichum novi-belgii* 'Porzellan' has dense, green foliage and lavender autumnal blossoms.

As Doug Croft points out, "Filler material provides background and substance to the cut flower arrangements. We cut back *Symphyotrichum novi-belgii* 'Porzellan' several times during the summer to keep the plants low and dense, and use the leafy stems as filler. *Dryopteris erythrosora* 'Brilliance' adds a reddish element to arrangements in spring (the fronds are reddish when they unfurl, turning green in the summer). Dwarf Korean goat's beard (*Aruncus aesthusifolius*) has fernlike foliage for greens as well as white flowers in midsummer. Asparagus foliage is finely textured and drapes elegantly over the edge of a vase. Branches of shrubs and trees from throughout the garden are also useful."

LEFT   Cool-season annual *Calendula officinalis* 'Radio' adds brilliant liveliness to the Cut Flower Garden.

RIGHT   An indispensible cut flower, *Verbena bonariensis* is a see-through annual topped with clusters of lavender flowers. In milder climates, the plant will overwinter, becoming more floriferous than the first-year seedlings.

Useful Annuals for Cut Flowers

Here is a list of some of our favorite cut flowers. All last well and provide a strong visual display in the vase.

Ageratum houstonianum—a lavender-blue self-seeder. 'Red Sea' is dark red-violet.

Alcea spp.—grows tall, with a friendly, old-fashioned feel.

Amaranthus hypochondriacus—has bold, feathery spikes.

Ammi spp.—looks like Queen Anne's lace but has more longevity as a cut flower.

Celosia spicata—great fresh or dry.

Consolida ajacis —delphinium relative that is a clear blue self-sower.

Cosmos spp.—two of our favorites are 'Purity' (white) and 'Rubenza' (wine red).

Helianthus annuus—has a wide selection of colors, heights, and flower sizes.

Rudbeckia hirta—we like 'Cappuccino', 'Kelvedon Star', and 'Prairie Sun'.

Scabiosa atropurpurea 'Ace of Spades'—boasts attractive burgundy flowers.

Salvia sclarea var. *turkestanica*—a biennial with bold silvery leaves and purplish flowers.

Zinnia spp.—have strong stems and come in a vast array of colors and sizes. 'Orange King' (soft orange), 'Canary Bird' (yellow), and 'Oriole' (deep orange) grow to 3 feet.

TOP   *Rudbeckia subtomentosa* 'Henry Eilers' offers plenty of yellow, fluted flowers for lavish bouquets.

BOTTOM   Towering up to 8 feet, *Helianthus maximiliani* 'Santa Fe' is the last of the perennial sunflowers to bloom. It reliably makes a spectacular show regardless of a dry or wet autumn.

Hollyhocks (*Alcea* spp.) offer a relaxed, cottage-garden nuance and make excellent cut flowers.

Self-Sowers

Self-sowing plants are the ultimate in relaxed gardening. Eric Hsu likens them to "cracked imperfections of a ceramic vessel. They prevent the garden from being too precious or too contrived. You plant or sow them once and they are part of your garden forever." Self-sowers fill seasonal holes in planting beds. Doug Croft sprinkles poppy seeds around bluebeard (*Caryopteris* ×*clandonensis*) and Russian sage (*Perovskia atriplicifolia*). Both are slow to leaf out in the spring and are notoriously unattractive until late June. Poppies germinate better with some cold, so he likes to sow the seeds on top of a light snow. He mixes the seed with damp, coarse sand to make it easier to see where the seeds land and make the planting less thick.

When getting started with self-sowers, give them bare ground to get established. Throw seed where you want the plants, or plant young seedlings. Most self-sowers germinate best when there is direct contact of the seed and the soil. Self-sowers can be weedy and we thin them mercilessly. Mulching suppresses weeds and cannot distinguish between wanted and unwanted seedlings. Where weed seed is abundant, mulch heavily first and then sow desired seeds.

The Rock Ledge is Joe Henderson's great experiment with self-sowers. He collects the seeds of *Papaver rhoeas* in summer when they

LEFT   The clear white *Cosmos bipinnatus* 'Purity' is a staff favorite for cut flowers. Regular deadheading of unsightly, spent flowers prolongs and improves its display.

RIGHT   *Helianthus annuus* 'Prado Red' is a dark mahogany-red sunflower that goes well with brighter colors either in the garden or in a floral arrangement. It is multiflowering, meaning that cutting one flower does not spell the plant's demise.

ripen and immediately sprinkles them over the hillside. In the Rock Ledge's first year, he used masses of the poppies and two umbellifers (*Daucus carota* 'Dara' and *Orlaya grandiflora*) to give the area a feeling of maturity. *Daucus* is the common Queen Anne's lace, but the cultivar 'Dara' has wine-colored florets. Not all the seeds come true to color, giving a mixture of pink and white. *Orlaya* is a gem Joe saw growing along the roadside in Montenegro. The creamy white flowers have petals shaped like pieces from a Calder mobile. The large flower clusters seem to cover the 15-inch-high plants. As he thins seedlings of self-sowers, he moves them to other beds and shares with others. Joe's other self-sowers include *Muscari azureum* for early spring and *Leucanthemum vulgare*, with its daisy flowers in mid-spring, followed by the tall and architectural *Verbascum olympicum* and then *Ratibida pinnata*, which loves the summer sun.

Breadseed poppy (*Papaver somniferum*) produces the poppy seed of cakes and bagels and has an unfortunate reputation in the drug trade. The most common form is double flowered and pink. Seedlings are almost impossible to transplant (unless grown as plugs), so we sow them where we want them. Larkspur (*Consolida ajacis*) and bachelor's buttons (*Centaurea cyanus*) are blue-flowered self-sowers and make

LEFT   White lace flower (*Orlaya grandiflora*), an endangered Cretan wildflower, has flat umbels of pristine white flowers atop finely dissected foliage. Fall-sown plants are larger than spring-sown ones and they flower longer.

RIGHT   From a single sowing, *Daucus carota* 'Dara' has exploded throughout the Rock Ledge. This pink- to wine-colored variant of the naturalized Queen Anne's lace is also an excellent cut flower.

CLOCKWISE FROM TOP LEFT "Ink" blotches are imprinted on ladybird poppy (*Papaver commutatum*) in a chic combination of red and black. We make autumn sowings, carefully prick out seedlings into individual narrow pots, and plant them out early before the ground freezes. Given protective snow cover, the plants survive to become large rosettes of downy foliage.

The beautiful Asian angelica (*Angelica gigas*) would not appear out of a place in a sci-fi horror flick, with its sinister maroon coloring, the podlike buds, and dense umbel structure.

Each breadseed poppy (*Papaver somniferum*) seedpod contains hundreds of tiny black seeds ready to disperse at the first rupture.

Because of its noxious weed status in some states, Scotch thistle (*Onopordum acanthium*) needs careful monitoring, but is carefully considered at Chanticleer for its architectural stature. Seedlings are rigorously edited.

spectacular cut flowers. Collect the seeds and disperse them exactly where you want them.

It isn't just annuals that self-sow. Native purplestem angelica (*Angelica atropurpurea*) and Asian angelica (*A. gigas*) are robust biennials whose seedlings start in late summer (in sun or shade) and bloom the following summer. Both angelicas have strong architecture and reach about 5 feet in height in part shade. The Asian species has reddish stems and burgundy, podlike buds unfurling into large dark red umbels up to 8 inches across in summer. It's useful at the back of a border or on the edge of the path where you can see pollinating insects feasting on its nectar-rich flowers up close. It likes a moist, well-drained, rich soil, and part shade. *Phacelia bipinnatifida* is a native biennial useful for its quick cover of shady areas. It germinates in the summer, producing only leaves, and then grows to 12 to 15 inches the next spring, covered with purple flowers with a display similar to geraniums.

Milk thistle (*Silybum marianum*) and Scotch thistle (*Onopordum acanthium*) are sculptural biennials for sunny spots with wicked spines on their leaves. Banned as invasive weeds in some states (but not Pennsylvania), we use them carefully and only allow a few seeds to ripen. Perennial Japanese primrose (*Primula japonica*) gives a blast of late-spring color in part shade and self-sows where there is no competition, especially in moist areas. *Verbena bonariensis* is a short-lived perennial that self-sows and blooms with showy but small purple flowers throughout the summer. *Thermopsis caroliniana*, *Echinacea*, *Asclepias*, and *Mertensia virginica* are native perennials that self-sow. *Echinacea* and *Asclepias* can become a bit weedy, but there rarely are enough bluebells (*Mertensia*). *Aquilegia canadensis* and *Lobelia cardinalis* are both short-lived perennials. We collect the seeds each year and toss them where we want more plants.

The bulblet bladder fern (*Cystopteris bulbifera*) produces bulblets on the underside of the leaf. The bulblets drop off the plant, root, and spread, just like seeds. You can easily collect and spread them yourself. Just toss where you want them to grow, including between rocks in a shady wall. It's a great perennial fern for shade, reaching a height of about 8 inches, with fronds up to 30 inches long. *Begonia grandis* subsp. *evansiana* is a perennial that looks like it shouldn't be hardy, but it is. It spreads by tiny bulbils that form in the leaf axil and then drop to the ground and sprout the following spring. Eventually, colonies form, emerging after most perennials have already leafed out.

Bamboos

Running bamboos, which invasively spread by underground runners, are thrilling yet scary in a garden. Because they are big, woody grasses, their leaves are finely textured, contrasting with bold stems. When we think of bamboo, we think of large stems (culms) that create

A surprisingly hardy species in a largely tender genus, *Begonia grandis* subsp. *evansiana* occasionally self-seeds, but forms large colonies rapidly through bulbils. These bulbils will become sizable begonia plants the following season.

fascinating forests of stems. None of the biggest bamboos is hardy for us at Chanticleer, but a large stand of *Phyllostachys aureosulcata* in Asian Woods is a treat to walk through. But, don't plant it! It runs and you will forever be trying to control it. Barriers are ineffective and we basically cut down the shoots and dig roots for control. The cultivar 'Spectabilis' has bright yellow stems and welcomes guests to the Asian Woods Restrooms. If it seems more polite, it's only because it is more recently planted. We are finding shoots of it coming up 20 feet away. *Phyllostachys vivax* 'Aureocaulis' has larger, yellow stems. It is impressive in its size, but is less hardy and dies to the ground every few years (but still runs like mad). Giant cane (*Arundinaria gigantea*) is a southeastern U.S. native that we are trying to get started in Bell's Woodland (yes, we never learn).

Several low, running bamboos make strong ground covers, but again, drive us crazy controlling them. *Sasa veitchii* grows to be 3 to 4 feet tall, with green leaves during the summer, becoming variegated as it is hit by frost. By the end of winter, the leaves are nearly white. We cut it to the ground every other year. Slightly lower, *Pleioblastus viridistriatus* (growing near the Ponds) tops at 2 feet and has bright yellow leaves. It makes a strong, golden show, but Joe Henderson digs around it every spring to keep it from taking over the entire area. Below the Chanticleer Terraces, *P. pygmaeus* has green leaves and reaches about 18 inches. We control it moderately well by mowing around it, but if you look at the mowed grass, you'll see that much of it is bamboo. Probably the only place these plants could safely be used would be in a parking lot or a street planting, surrounded by acres of paving.

There are clumping bamboos and they are attractive in their fountain effect. Sadly, their stems are thin and have nothing of the effect of the big bamboos. We grow several species of *Fargesia* and you can find their attractive clumps in Asian Woods.

THE SERPENTINE AND
THE VEGETABLE GARDENS

The type of gardening we do is first about beauty, but we also find joy in growing our own food. We do this 'edible landscaping' throughout the garden, but especially in the Vegetable Garden and in the Serpentine. All plants in the Vegetable Garden bear edibles and we harvest throughout the season, but we always keep the area looking good. Most of the produce is eaten by our staff. When we have a surplus of food, we share it with a local shelter. We plant the Serpentine with agronomic crops, which sometimes are not edible (such as linen and tobacco).

Taking the use of foliage repetition to another level, the Serpentine highlights the foliage, shape, and texture of agronomic crops. The area is named for its sinuous lines and was inspired by a curvaceous farm road at Tuscany's Villa La Foce, designed by Cecil Pinsent. Eric Hsu says, "The Serpentine is best viewed from afar, from the Chanticleer House Overlook or the Gravel Garden Arbor. Only then do its sinuous lines become clear, unobscured by the plantings at ground level. However, they are effective at ground level as the beds swirl toward you, hooking into the lawn."

We use 'Emerald Sentinel' junipers instead of tender Italian cypresses, and silver-leaved willows (*Salix alba* 'Britzensis') to mimic olive trees. These permanent components plus espaliered ginkgoes, bigleaf magnolia, and sugar maples provide the ballast against the temporal planting of the Serpentine.

Celebrating the aesthetics of agriculture, we have chosen crops such as sorghum, wheat, rye, barley, sunflowers, tobacco, soybeans, rapeseed, crimson clover, kale, flax, and sesame. Just as in an agricultural field, we rotate crops, with a grain following a legume. A seed drill ensures precise, even spacing, and hoeing controls the weeds. Most of the crops are composted rather than harvested, but the year we grew three cultivars of kale (*Brassica oleracea* 'Redbor', 'Russian Blue', 'Lacinato'), we ate all summer long. The colorful kale demonstrated itself as an ornamental vegetable as well as a health food. Eric Hsu pointed out the kale's colors tied well to purple-tinged 'Blue Heaven' little bluestem grass in front of the nearby willows. This cultivar retains its upright habit without the floppiness of the species, demanding full sun to thrive. Birds feast on the grain seeds, and the years we grew sunflowers, finches ate for weeks, as did hawks on the finches. The Serpentine planting is bigger than most home gardens, but think how effective even a 9-by-3-foot curvaceous line of flowers, foliage plants, or vegetables might be.

Originally, the area eroded in the winter with rainwater flooding in from the road above. Winter cover crops and a no-till program reduced soil erosion and increased the amount of organic matter in the soil.

Winter rye

Storm water slowed in detention basins under the willows, which are planted with American grasses to resemble a Tuscan meadow. The basins themselves are like rain gardens, flooding with water after rains and becoming desertlike in droughts. A suckering sedge (*Carex stricta*) and a clumping, evergreen rush (*Juncus effusus*) thrive in the deep part of the basins. Tufted hairgrass (*Deschampsia cespitosa*) and fox sedge (*Carex vulpinoidea*) grow well along the edges of the basins and in the uppermost basin that drains quickly.

ABOVE AND THE FOLLOWING FOUR PAGES
The Serpentine has seen many renditions of agronomic crops, including rye, cotton, sorghum, and kale.

Cotton on a muggy summer morning

Sorghum

Winter rye

Edibles

Vegetable gardens are as much foliage displays as they are food sources. Our 210-foot row of asparagus (*Asparagus officinalis* 'Jersey Knight') defines the southern boundary of the Cut Flower Garden like a 4-foot hedge and provides six weeks of fantastic eating in mid to late spring. 'Jersey Knight' is a male strain and rust resistant. We place attractive terra-cotta containers with lids (marketed as rhubarb forcing pots) over individual clumps of asparagus to block out light, resulting in succulent, clean, white asparagus. To the north, cold frames are often filled with vegetable seedlings as well as early and late-season crops of edibles, extending the harvest a month or more in spring and fall.

A low, wooden fence backed with wire mesh designates the Vegetable Garden. The fence keeps out rabbits and rodents. Deer are not a problem, because Chanticleer's garden acres are surrounded by deer fence. Besides discouraging hungry rabbits, the fence supports vines, such as hardy kiwi (*Actinidia arguta*), squashes, and gourds. 'Lunch Lady' gourd is an attractive mix of colors and warty appearance. Ridged luffa (*Luffa acutangula*) has prolific yellow flowers and produces scrubbing sponges in the fall. Scarlet runner bean, *Phaseolus coccineus*, has showy red flowers and tasty young beans. We've even espaliered *Solanum lycopersicum* 'Tigerella' tomatoes (red with orange stripes) on the fence.

Emma Seniuk plants the Vegetable Garden to be productive and attractive, with a different design each year. The season begins with cold-tolerant lettuces of various colors (*Lactuca sativa* 'Reine des Glaces' has a ruffled green leaf and *L. sativa* 'Forellenschluss' is a Romaine with mottled foliage), cilantro, onions, parsley, spinach, beets, chard, and arugula. We let arugula flower, finding the four-petaled, white blossoms attractive, tasty, and peppery. As spring warms, peas (including edible-pod types) climb supports of bamboo from Asian Woods. Climbing beans replace the peas as the summer begins.

Even though cabbages (*Brassica oleracea*) love cool weather, picking the large heads continues into summer. Zucchini (*Cucurbito pepo*) begins producing, and vining Malabar spinach (*Basella alba*) produces edible leaves on attractive vines. Some favorite tomatoes (*Solanum lycopersicum*) in our region for beauty and taste include 'Juane Peche' (small, tomentose, yellow fruits with a slight pink blush) and 'Blondkopfchen' (a profusion of flowers in early summer followed by a cascade of small, yellow fruits until frost).

We begin sowing flats of autumn crops in late summer for later transplanting. Vegetable gardens often look a bit rough in the fall, and newly planted crops keep it feeling vibrant. Spinach, lettuce, beets, and brassicas perform beautifully in the fall. Kohlrabi ('Kolibri' is a strong purple), kale, and Brussels sprouts continue producing after frost. 'Purple Perfection' red cabbage is attractive in the garden, in containers, and on the dinner table. Brussels sprouts taste best after frost.

Eaten raw or prepared like spinach in Asian cuisine, *Brassica juncea* 'Osaka Purple' asserts itself with large purple leaves in a seasonal spring display with *Antirrhinum majus* 'Playful Canary', *Corydalis flexuosa* 'Blue Panda', and *Nassella tenuissima*. 'Osaka Purple', a peppery mustard, bolts in the summer heat, producing attractive, tasty yellow flowers.

Most visitors are surprised at how beautiful asparagus (*Asparagus officinalis* 'Jersey Knight') plants can be. Here, the feathery "leaves," in fact modified stems, glisten silvery and create billowing textures across the length of the Cut Flower and Vegetable Gardens.

Our edibles are not limited to the Vegetable Garden. The Teacup Garden and Chanticleer Terraces feature cold-tolerant, colored-leaved Chinese cabbages, mustard greens, lettuces, and chards for color in the spring plantings. All do well in the ground and in containers. *Lactuca sativa* 'Lollo Rossa' is a highly ornamental red leaf lettuce. Its frilled, deep red leaves look fantastic as filler between spring annuals or at the feet of tulips. 'Lollo Bionda' is similar but green. The large, textured leaves of purple mustard *Brassica juncea* 'Red Giant' keep their burgundy color. Swiss chard tolerates the summer heat, and its vibrant colorful stems and leaves remain showy until November. Rosemary, sage, lavender, and other herbs love the warm sunny heat of the terraces. Bay trees (*Laurus nobilis*) in pots serve as accents, as do olives and figs; all three go inside for the winter. Near the Teacup Garden, we place containers high atop courtyard walls; vining edibles give a totally different effect when planted above the viewer. Cucumbers, tomatoes, beans, and Italian squash (*Cucurbita pepo* 'Trombetta d'Albenga') gracefully drape down the walls.

'Issai' hardy kiwi (*Actinidia arguta* 'Issai') fruits without a male pollinator, but production is higher in the presence of male companions. Its tasty fruit has the same flavor and texture as the supermarket kiwi (*A. deliciosa*), but lacks the fuzzy skin. We train the rambunctious shoots around the perimeter of the Vegetable Garden fence.

The Vegetable Garden approaches its full summer harvest as tomatoes begin to ripen.

LEFT   The interior leaves of Savoy cabbage 'Deadon' (*Brassica oleracea* var. *sabauda* 'Deadon') reveal a rich magenta color that intensifies with colder temperatures.

RIGHT   *Cucurbita maxima* 'Red Kuri', also known as 'Orange Hokkaido', is decked out in a festive color for Halloween and is good for pumpkin pies.

OPPOSITE   Tomatoes, cucumbers, and sweet potatoes fill and cascade from the containers and walls near the Teacup Garden, bringing vegetables to eye level and reach.

Afterword

Whether or not gardening is art doesn't really matter. Gardening is what we do because we must. We put everything we have into Chanticleer, making it personal and unique, and we aim to make our garden the absolute best we can. Chanticleer is a result of its location, topography, climate, and most of all, the people who built it and those who continue to develop it. We garden like it is our own and treat those who visit like personal guests. We hope to inspire others to garden more freely and passionately, as we do.

Our site's features guide our design, and we integrate the structures and garden as one. Themes tie the various areas together and we change gradually rather than with grand landscape designs. We love plants and keep trying new ones. Design brings the cacophony of plants into harmony, and combining plants into ensembles is more important than what the individual plants are.

In some areas, repetition of a plant holds together a diversity of plants, such as grasses weaving their way through the perennials of the Tennis Court. In other areas, such as in the Ruin Meadow, we use a large mass of one species, *Sporobolus heterolepis*, and add interest by dotting in coneflowers, cypresses, and maples. In both cases, the grasses hold the composition together, as the strings do in an orchestral piece.

In an orchestra, the woodwinds may take center stage for a while, then the brasses take over. Likewise, areas of the garden have their periods of brilliance, followed by moments of calm. The Bulb Meadow comes into bloom at various times, followed by the green and tan of long grasses. The Creek Garden bursts into the blue of camassias in mid-spring and then is green until autumn color grabs attention. The Chanticleer Terraces rest in the winter, following their exuberance in spring, summer, and fall.

By gardening to please ourselves, we have developed a personal garden we hope our guests enjoy. Aiming to please ourselves is not as narcissistic as it seems. To continue with the musical theme, a composer writes the best piece she can and keeps improving it until she pleases herself. She doesn't write for the audience, but obviously hopes the audience will love it. In your own garden, trust your instincts. Design to please yourself and make the garden your personal expression. You cannot serve two masters, nor can your garden. It needs vision and a strong leader to be good.

Enough discussion. Let's all get back to gardening.

As if to bless the garden's 100th anniversary in 2013, a Rhode Island barred rock rooster decided to make Asian Woods its temporary home. His surprise arrival symbolizes the intimate playfulness that makes Chanticleer a riveting garden for all who visit.

Suggested Reading

Brickell, Christopher, and David Joyce. *RHS Pruning and Training.* New York: DK Publishing, 2011.

Bruce, Harold. *Winterthur in Bloom.* New York: Chanticleer Press, 1968.

———. *How to Grow Wildflowers and Wild Shrubs and Trees in Your Own Garden.* New York: Alfred A. Knopf, 1976.

Chatto, Beth. *The Green Tapestry.* London, UK: HarperCollins, 1990.

———. *The Dry Garden.* London, UK: Orion, 2012.

Coleman, Eliot. *Four-Season Harvest.* Danvers, MA: Chelsea Green Publishing, 1999.

Culp, David. *The Layered Garden.* Portland, OR: Timber Press, 2012.

Dirr, Michael A. *Manual of Woody Landscape Plants.* Champaign, IL: Stipes, 2009.

Gilman, Edward F. *An Illustrated Guide to Pruning.* Clifton Park, NY: Delmar, Dengage Learning, 2012.

Hanson, Richard, and Freidrich Stahl. *Perennials and Their Garden Habitats.* Portland, OR: Timber Press, 1993.

Higgins, Adrian, and Rob Cardillo (photography). *Chanticleer: A Pleasure Garden.* Philadelphia, PA: University of Pennsylvania Press, 2011.

Hinkley, Daniel J. *The Explorer's Garden.* Portland, OR: Timber Press, 2009.

Keswick, Maggie. *The Chinese Garden: History, Art and Architecture.* Cambridge, MA: Harvard University Press, 2003.

Kostof, Spiro, Richard Tobias, and Gregory Castillo. *A History of Architecture: Settings and Rituals.* New York: Oxford University Press, 1995.

Kuck, Lorraine E. *The Art of Japanese Gardens.* New York: The John Day Co., 1941.

Lloyd, Christopher. *The Well-Tempered Garden.* New York: Random House, 1985.

———. *Gardener Cook.* London, UK: Frances Lincoln Publishers, 2001.

———. *Succession Planting for Adventurous Gardeners*. London, UK: BBC Books, 2005.

———. *Succession Planting for Year-Round Pleasure*. Portland, OR: Timber Press, 2005.

Lloyd, Christopher, and Erica Hunningher. *Meadows*. Portland, OR: Timber Press, 2004.

Nicholson, Nigel. *Portrait of a Marriage*. New York: Atheneum, 1973.

Nitschke, Guenther. *Japanese Gardens*. Cologne, Germany: Taschen, 2003.

Ogden, Lauren Springer, and Rob Proctor. *Passionate Gardening: Good Advice for Challenging Climates*. Golden, CO: Fulcrum Publishing, 2000.

Ogden, Scott, and Lauren Springer Ogden. *Plant-Driven Design: Creating Gardens That Honor Plants, Place, and Spirit*. Portland, OR: Timber Press, 2008.

Ost, Daniel. *Invitations*. Tielt, Belgium: Lannoo Publishers, 2003.

———. *Invitations 2*. Tielt, Belgium: Lannoo Publishers, 2010.

Oudolf, Piet, and Noel Kingsbury. *Designing with Plants*. Portland, OR: Timber Press, 1999.

Pearson, Dan. *Spirit: Garden Inspiration*. London, UK: Fuel Publishing, 2011.

Robinson, William, and Rick Darke. *The Wild Garden*. Expanded edition. Portland, OR: Timber Press, 2009.

Sternberg, Guy. *Native Trees for North American Landscapes*. Portland, OR: Timber Press, 2004.

Taylor, Gordon, and Guy Cooper. *Gardens of Obsession: Eccentric and Extravagant Visions*. London, UK: Cassell, 1999.

Wiley, Keith. *On the Wild Side: Experiments in the New Naturalism*. Portland, OR: Timber Press, 2004.

Winterrowd, Wayne. *Annuals and Tender Plants for North American Gardens*. New York: Random House, 2004.

Wyman, Donald. *Wyman's Gardening Encyclopedia*. New York: Scribner, 1987.

Index

Arisaema sikokianum, 275
Arisaema triphyllum, 275
Aristolochia/aristolochias, 222, 229
Aristolochia gigantea, 222, 229
Aristolochia macrophylla, 229
Aristolochia manshuriensis, 227, 229
Aristolochia tomentosa, 229
Artemisia 'Powis Castle', 79
Art Nouveau influences, 103, 104
arts and crafts, role of, 98–99, 101–104, 106
arugula, 308
aruncus, 271
Aruncus aesthusifolius, 291
Arundinaria gigantea, 300
Asclepias, 299
Asclepias tuberosa, 42, 280
ash trees, 16, 128
Asian angelica, 296, 299
Asian maple, 235
Asian sweet autumn clematis, 222
Asian Woods
    bamboo theme, 66–67
    development, 68
    plant list box, 106
    rustic bench, 101, 103
    as shade garden, 42, 264, 267
    trees, 64–66, 140
    watering methods, 290
Asian Woods Restrooms, 58, 60, 103
asparagus, 308, 310
asparagus foliage, 282, 291
Asparagus officinalis 'Jersey Knight', 308, 310
asters, 88, 89, 291
Aster tataricus, 286
Astilboides tabularis, 215
Aucuba japonica
    'Picturata', 269
    'Salicifolia', 269
    'Variegata', 269
aucubas, 269
Austrian pine, 146

autumn-blooming bulbs, 250, 259
autumn crocus, 259
autumn fern, 252
autumn fruit displays, 275
avalanche lily, 277
azaleas, 186

B

Baccharis halimifolia, 200, 201, 286
bachelor's buttons, 295, 299
Baird, Mara, 61
bald cypresses, 104, 145
bamboo
    as Asian Woods theme, 66–67
    canes as edging and fencing, 67, 286
    ground-covering, 152, 300
    invasive spreading and controlling of, 299–300
    as plant supports, 106, 308
Bambusa ceramicus 'Chanticleerensis' sculptures, 104
banana
    'Black Thai', 53–54
    Japanese, 38
    overwintering, 38, 54, 55
Baptisia, 154
bark color and texture, 159–162
barley, 302
Barr, Peter, 250
Basella alba, 308
bay tree, 310
beans, 308, 310
beauty bush, 186, 188
bed edges as integrating features, 61
beeches, 92, 95, 97, 118, 128, 252
beets, 70, 308
Begonia/begonias, 48
    'Lotusland', 48
    'Sparks Will Fly', 252
Begonia boliviensis 'Bonfire', 70
Begonia grandis, 114, 118

Begonia grandis subsp. *evansiana*, 299
Bell's Run, 63, 259–260
Bell's Woodland, 18, 24, 68, 92–95, 97
benches, 101, 103
Bessera elegans, 245
Better Homes and Gardens, 20
Betula papyrifera, 43
biennials, 280, 286, 292, 299
bigleaf magnolia, 169, 302
birds
    attractants, 115, 212, 224, 279
    diversity of habitats for, 158
    food sources, 149, 158, 166, 169, 172, 286, 302
    at the ponds, 212, 215
bishop's flower, 250
Bismarckia nobilis, 78
black cotton, 54, 55
blackhaw viburnum, 192
black sweet potato vine, 54
black walnut trees, 12, 128, 131
Bletchley Park, 14
Bletilla striata, 272
bloom, sequence of. *See* succession of bloom
bluebeard, 294
bluebells, 299
blue camassias, 62
blue spruce, 228
bluestem, 122, 286, 302
Boehmeria, 271
Boehmeria spicata, 271
Bog by the Ponds, 37, 41
borders
    Long Border, 125, 150, 152
    Winter Shrub Border, 6, 144, 145, 249, 254, 280, 286
Borie, Charles, 12
bottlebrush buckeye, 121
boxwoods, 115, 182, 183
Brassica juncea
    'Osaka Purple', 308
    'Red Giant', 69, 80, 310
Brassica napus var. *pabularia*
    'Red Russian', 80

proportion in mixed plantings, 250
to rest the senses, 202, 204,
212, 215–216
simplicity, 121
site-shaped, 36–39, 42, 92,
317
as solution, 73
symphonic harmony as
metaphor, 61, 62
See also naturalistic design
Deutzia gracilis 'Chardonnay
Pearls', 154
Dianthus 'Mountain Mist',
110
Diascia/diascias, 80
'Flirtation Orange', 79
Dichondra argentea, 78
'Silver Falls', 86
digging, hand vs. rototilling,
29
Digitalis, 154, 280
dioecious plants, 118, 200
Diospyros virginiana, 162
Dixie wood fern, 51, 132
dogwood blossoms as artistic
motif, 104, 169
dogwood stems and branches,
52–53, 70, 81, 140
dogwood trees, 64, 169, 172,
184, 221, 250
Donahue, Marcia, 23, 99,
101, 104
Draba ramosissima, 115
dragon's breath, 80
drinking fountains, 12, 98,
101
Dryopteris, 269
Dryopteris ×*australis*, 51, 132
Dryopteris erythrosora 'Brilliance', 132, 252, 291
Dutch crocuses, 243
Dutchman's pipe, 222, 229
dwarf aruncus, 271
dwarf hemlocks, 200
dwarf Korean goat's beard,
291

E

eastern redbud, 95
eastern red cedar, 106
eastern white pine, 147
Echeveria 'Perle Von Nürnberg', 55
Echinacea, 116, 299
Echinacea purpurea, 280
Echinacea tennesseensis, 116
edging, 61, 66–67
edible plants, 302, 308, 310
Elegia tectorum, 70
elephant ears, 53, 54
Emilia coccinea, 109
Emily's House, 14, 15, 18, 60,
125
endangered plant species,
116, 295
Enemion biternatum, 277
English ivy, 221
Ensete ventricosum 'Maurelli',
55
Entrance Pavilion
container groupings, 82, 83
design, 58, 60–61
railings, 103, 221
environmentally friendly
practices, 28, 149, 202,
204. *See also* storm water
management
ephemerals, shade-blooming,
277–279
ephemerals, spring, 31, 92,
121, 174, 241, 264, 280
Epilobium canum, 115
Epimedium/epimediums, 118,
264, 267
'Amber Queen', 267
Epimedium perralderianum,
118
Epimedium rhizomatosum, 118
Epimedium stellulatum, 267
Epimedium ×*versicolor* 'Sulphureum', 267, 268
Epimedium ×*warleyense*
'Orangekönigin', 267
Epimedium wushanense, 267
Epimedium ×*youngianum*
'Niveum', 134

Eranthis, 238
Eranthis hyemalis, 238
Eremurus, 280, 282
Eremurus himalaicus, 115
Erigeron pulchellus, 250
Eryngium amethystinum, 50
Erysimum, 70, 81
'Winter Joy', 139
'Winter Orchid', 139
Erysimum cheiri 'Blood Red',
70
Erythronium 'Pagoda', 277
Erythronium revolutum, 277
Erythronium tuolumnense, 277
Eschscholzia californica, 89,
156
espaliers
as contrast to relaxed look,
121
in Cut Flower Garden, 233,
235
as hedges, 233, 235
to highlight blooms, 20,
231, 234
pruning, 231
at the Ruin, 44, 174, 186,
232
tomatoes on a fence, 308
on walls, 44, 135, 149, 166,
232
Euonymus alatus, 92
Euphorbia amygdaloides 'Ruby
Glow', 70
Euphorbia 'Blackbird', 71
Euphorbia characias 'Glacier
Blue', 71
Euphorbia cotinifolia, 80
Euphorbia epithymoides, 90
Euphorbia hypericifolia 'Dia-
mond Frost', 54
Euphorbia ×*martini* 'Tiny
Tim', 79
European beeches, 128
European larch, 145
Eurybia divaricata, 274
Eustoma grandiflorum, 156
'Mariachi Sapphire Blue
Chip', 50
Eutrochium maculatum 'Gate-
way', 216, 282

evergreen shrubs, 182
evergreen trees, 140, 144, 146, 149, 152
exposures. *See* light exposures

F

Fagus grandifolia, 159
Fagus sylvatica, 128
false daphne, 176
false larch, 145
false rue anemone, 277
Fargesia, 300
fencing
  around the Waterwheel, 103
  bamboo, 67, 286
  cut willow hoops, 135, 138
  deer, 44, 103, 308
  to discourage rabbits and rodents, 308
  as vine supports, 308
fernleaf beech, 128
ferns
  autumn fern, 252
  bulblet bladder fern, 62, 63, 299
  Christmas fern, 132
  as companions, 270
  in cool, moist areas, 43
  Dixie wood fern, 51, 132
  fronds as inspiration, 103
  as mantel decoration, 48
  in a native plant garden, 92
  as shade plants, 264, 299
fescues, 202, 204, 208
Festuca idahoensis, 89
Ficaria verna, 92
Fiddlehead Path, 62, 63
fig trees, 310
firecracker plant, 80
firs, 146
flax, 302
flooding and erosion, 24
Florida anise, 176
Flower Garden, 20
flowering cherry trees, 134, 159, 163–164, 166, 250
flowering dogwoods, 64, 169
flowering quince 'Jet Trail', 235

flowery lawn, 115, 204, 209, 262
Foeniculum vulgare 'Purpureum', 53, 55, 70, 109, 286
foliage
  asparagus, 282, 291
  autumn, 159
  as constant among fluctuating colors, 280
  displays in vegetable gardens, 308
  importance for color, 152
  repetition with agronomic crops, 302
  for shade, 264, 267–269
  shrubs for colorful, 184–186
  yellow-themed, 152
  See also leaves as artistic motif
foot traffic, 132, 202
forget-me-nots, 250
Foster hollies, 149
fountain motif, 78
fox sedge, 303
foxtail lilies, 115, 282
Fraxinus americana, 128
Fraxinus pennsylvanica, 128
fringe tree, 169, 174
Fritillaria meleagris, 238, 242, 250
fritillaries, 238, 250
frosty elm, 235
furniture
  aesthetic connection to garden, 103
  benches, 101, 103
  created by gardeners, 98, 101, 103, 106
  stone, 45
  See also chairs
fuschia, 115

G

Galanthus elwesii, 238
Galanthus nivalis, 238
  'Flore Pleno', 238
gardeners
  artistic vision, 9
  artistry of, 98, 101, 103, 106

collaboration, 36, 58, 106, 108–109
  views on color, 156–157
gardening as art, 9–10
"gardening without a net," 10
garden rooms, 36, 44–45, 47
"geophytes," 236
Geum 'Starkers Magnificum', 89
Geum 'Totally Tangerine', 79
giant hyssop, 64, 88
giant pussy willow, 135
giant scabious, 156
Ginkgo biloba / ginkgoes, 302
  'Princeton Sentry', 233, 235
Gladiolus 'Atom', 245, 249
Gladiolus communis subsp. *byzantinus* 'Cruentus', 280
Gladiolus murielae, 54
Glaucidium palmatum, 10
glider, 101, 106
globeflowers, 280
golden club, 215
golden larches, 145
Gomphocarpus physocarpus, 24
Gomphrena/gomphrenas, 290
  'Fireworks', 53, 55, 290
Gomphrena haageana 'Strawberry Fields', 290
Goodman, Samuel, 15
Gossypium herbaceum 'Nigra', 54, 55
gourd 'Lunch Lady', 308
grape hyacinths, 250, 254
grape vines, 229
grasses
  annual, as companions, 262, 263
  controlled burning of, 204, 208
  as repeating elements, 64, 76, 317
  textural contrast between long and mown, 207, 208
  that function as hedges, 76, 262
  turf, 202, 204, 208
  as unifying element, 76
grassleaf sweet flag, 215

light exposures
  north-facing, 37, 41
  south-facing, 37, 38, 78,
    204
Lighty, Richard, 267
Ligularia fischeri, 273
lilies, 252–253
  African Queen strain, 252
  'Barcelona', 252
  orienpet, 252
  'Saltarello', 252
  'Scheherazade', 252
  'Sixth Sense', 252
Lilium, 252
  'Brunello', 252
  'Casa Blanca', 252
  'Citronella', 252
  'Swansea', 252
Lilium canadense, 252
Lilium grayi, 252
Lilium lancifolium, 252, 253
Lilium michiganense, 252
Lilium philadelphicum, 252
Lilium pumilum, 252
Lilium superbum, 252
lindens, 128
lion's tail, 80
Liriodendron tulipifera, 159
liriope, 73
lisianthus, 156
little bluestem, 286
  'Blue Heaven', 122, 302
Lobelia cardinalis, 277, 282,
    299
loblolly pines, 146
Lobularia maritima 'Clear
    Crystal Purple Shade', 69
Loebner magnolia, 169
Long Border, 125, 150, 152
longstalk holly, 150
lotuses, 212, 282
  'Mrs. Perry D. Slocum',
    157, 280
Luffa acutangula, 308
Lunaria annua, 250
  'Variegata', 250
Lupinus, 280
Lychnis flos-cuculi 'Jenny', 250
Lycoris squamigera, 259
Lysichiton, 277

Lysichiton americanus, 277
Lysichiton camtschatcensis, 277

M

Maclura pomifera, 103
Magnolia acuminata, 169
Magnolia acuminata var. *sub-
    cordata*, 169
Magnolia denudata, 169
Magnolia grandiflora, 149, 235
  'Bracken's Brown Beauty',
    149
  'Edith Bogue', 149, 235
  espaliers, 235
  'Little Gem', 149, 235
Magnolia ×*kewensis* 'Wada's
    Memory', 122
Magnolia ×*loebneri*, 169
Magnolia macrophylla, 169,
    170
Magnolia macrophylla subsp.
    ashei, 169
Magnolia/magnolias, 118, 121,
    122, 149, 169, 170, 302
  'Elizabeth', 169, 170, 254
  'Judy Zuk', 122, 169
  'Lois', 169, 171
Magnolia sieboldii, 243
Magnolia ×*soulangeana*, 169
Magnolia stellata, 169
Magnolia virginiana, 150
  'Green Shadow' (formerly
    'Green Bay'), 149
  'Henry Hicks', 152
  'Moonglow' (formerly 'Jim
    Wilson'), 152
maintenance
  gardens with varying
    requirements, 24
  as guiding principle, 28
  lasting structures to reduce
    costs, 29, 31
  lawns, 202, 204, 208–209
  mosses, 97
  trees, 18, 132
Malabar spinach, 308
Malus spp., 166
  'Donald Wyman', 166
  'Indian Summer', 166

  'Jewelberry', 166
  'Snowdrift', 166, 167
maples, 20, 317
marigolds, 156
martagon lilies, 252
master plan, 11, 61
McCabe, Marty, 104
meadows
  Bulb Meadow, 118, 128,
    208, 259
  flowery lawns, 115, 204,
    209, 262
  grasses for a meadow-like
    effect, 262, 303
  most photographed, 204
  Ruin Meadow, 99, 151, 204,
    208
  stylized meadow container
    planting, 55
  transforming grassy areas
    into, 209
  as wild perennial beds, 204
Meconopsis 'Lingholm', 81
Mediterranean plants, 39
Melianthus major, 71
Melinis nerviglumis, 88
Mertensia, 299
Mertensia virginica, 250, 277,
    299
metalworking, 103
Metasequoia glyptostroboides,
    122, 125, 144, 159
  'Gold Rush', 145
metasequoias, 145, 208
Mexican feather grass, 81, 121
microclimates, 37–39, 41–43,
    97, 144, 204, 235
milk thistle, 299
milkweed, 88
million bells, 83
Minder House, 14–15, 18
Minder Woods, 122, 150, 191,
    244, 269
Monarda citriodora, 282
mondo grass, 267
Morrison, Darrel, 92
mosses, 92, 94, 97
Moss Walk, 43
mountain laurel, 176, 180
mowing

controlling invasive plants, 300

controlling weed and tree seedlings, 209

coordinating with bulb bloom, 259

environmental considerations, 28, 202

increasing mulched areas for less, 122

lawns, 202, 204, 208–209

paths, 118

rationale for lack of, 209

Mt. Cuba Center, 267

Muhlenbergia capillaris, 121, 286

mulching
  around trees, 122
  for weed control, 204, 294
  when establishing self-sowers, 294
  when overwintering new bulbs, 236

Musa basjoo, 38

Muscari armeniacum, 236, 250, 251, 254

Muscari azureum, 295

Muscari botryoides, 254

mustard, 80, 308

mustard greens, 69, 70, 310

Myosotis sylvatica, 250

N

naked lily, 259

Napaea dioica, 282

Narcissus cantabricus, 250

Narcissus/narcissus, 81, 254
  'Actaea', 254
  'Barrett Browning', 254, 257
  'Bravoure', 254
  'Elka', 259
  'February Gold', 254
  'February Silver', 254
  'Hawera', 215, 236, 250, 251, 259
  'Ice Follies', 254
  'Ice Wings', 254
  'Jet Fire', 254

'Peeping Tom', 254
'Salome', 254
'Tête-à-Tête', 254

narrowleaf cattail, 215, 217

Nassella tenuissima, 81, 121, 280

Nasturtium officinalis, 216

native plant garden. *See* Bell's Woodland

naturalistic design
  achieving with evergreen screens, 144
  at Chanticleer Terraces, 115
  editing for a "wild" garden, 88, 89
  through repetition, simplicity, and diversity, 121
  for trees of the same species, 122
  See also meadows

Nectaroscordum siculum subsp. *bulgaricum*, 245

Nelumbo, 212
  'Momo Botan', 215
  'Mrs. Perry D. Slocum', 212

Nelumbo lutea, 212

Nelumbo nucifera, 212

Nemesia, 81

Nepeta, 280

nettle family, 271

Nicotiana langsdorffii, 70

Nigella damascena 'Miss Jekyll', 284

ninebark, 184

nurse logs, 97

Nymphaea
  'Arc-en-Ciel', 212
  'James Brydon', 212
  'Pygmaea Helvola', 212
  'Texas Dawn', 212, 214

nyssas, 128

Nyssa sylvatica, 159

O

oak-leaf hydrangea, 199

oaks, 14, 16, 92, 97, 133

Olea europaea 'Arbequina', 83

olive trees, 79, 83, 310

onions, 308

Onopordum acanthium, 297, 299

ophiopogon, 269

Ophiopogon planiscapus 'Nigrescens', 267

orange bromeliad, 80

Orchard, 166–167, 174, 207

Orchard Bulb Lawn, 254

orchids, 272, 273

organic practices
  fertilizers, 202, 204
  pest control, 149

Oriental lilies, 252

Origanum vulgare 'Aureum', 55

Orlaya, 295

Orlaya grandiflora, 75, 295

ornamental onions, 76, 243, 245

ornamental vegetables, 302

Orontium aquaticum, 215, 218

Osage orange bench, 101

Osteospermum/osteospermums, 80, 81
  'Serenity Bronze', 79

overwintering
  bananas, 38, 54, 55
  bulbs, 236
  in cold frames, 81, 286
  Gladiolus communis subsp. *byzantinus* 'Cruentus', 280
  Himalayan blue poppies, 81
  Rhododendron 'Mary Fleming', 176
  succulents in the ground, 90
  Verbena bonariensis, 291
  winter rye, 262

owls, 158, 159

oxblood lily, 56

Oxydendrum arboreum, 128, 159

Oxypetalum caeruleum, 78

P

Paeonia 'Cytherea', 280, 290

Paeonia japonica, 275

contemporary, 56
desert, 78
integrating function of, 36, 61, 317
old-fashioned effect, 53
stylized meadow, 55
tropical, 52, 54
See also color themes
Thermopsis caroliniana, 283, 299
Thermopsis/thermopsis, 152, 282
Thermopsis villosa, 154
The Wild Garden (Robinson), 250
Thuja occidentalis, 144
  'Yellow Ribbon', 154
Thuja plicata, 114, 144
  'Atrovirens', 149
Thuja/thujas, 144
  'Green Giant', 144
thyme, 88
Thymus, 280
Thymus praecox subsp. *arcticus*, 110
tiarella, 94
tiger lilies, 252
Tilia americana, 122
Tilia tomentosa, 118, 131
Tithonia rotundifolia, 286
toad lily, 118
tobacco, 302
tomatoes, 308, 310, 314
"tommies," 238, 243
touch-me-not, 274
trailing rosemary, 53
transitional plantings as integrating features, 61
transitions
  blending zones, 36, 61, 64, 122
  seasonal, 69–71, 159
trees
  autumn color, 159
  bark color and texture, 159–162
  causes of death, 18
  choosing young, 134
  as container accents, 310
  flowering, 163–164, 166–167, 169–171, 174

groves, 16, 66, 97, 122, 125, 147, 159, 174
importance in Chanticleer landscape, 18
maintenance, 18, 132
most commented on, 122
nuisance aspects, 128
oldest, 12
planting under, 122, 128, 132–134
replacing, 134
root systems, 132, 134
shade, 122, 128
soil considerations, 128
for suburban neighborhoods, 122
training for strong branching structure, 132
See also conifers; espaliers; evergreens
tree yuccas, 200
Tricyrtis, 118, 274
Tricyrtis hirta 'Variegata', 277
Trillium grandiflorum, 277, 278, 279
Trillium sessile, 277
Trillium/trilliums, 277
trumpet lilies, 252
Tsuga canadensis, 149
  'Pendula', 149
tufted hairgrass, 303
Tulipa
  'Apeldoorn', 18, 286
  'Fire Wings', 79
  'Maytime', 70
  'Menton', 70
  'Negrita', 286
  'Orange Princess', 79
  'Oratorio', 90
  'Pink Impression', 18
  'Rem's Favourite', 286
  'White Triumphator', 51
Tulipa acuminata, 236
Tulipa clusiana, 236
  'Lady Jane', 236, 250, 251
Tulipa linifolia, 236
tulips, 18, 69, 70, 80, 115
  'Black Parrot', 69, 70
  companions, 250
  Darwin, 236

extending the bloom season, 236
grouping for continuity, 286
  'Jan Reus', 250
  'National Velvet', 250
tuliptrees, 92, 95, 97, 118, 128
turf, 132, 133
turf grass, 122, 202, 204, 208
Typha angustifolia, 215, 217
Typha minima, 215

U

Ulmus parvifolia 'Frosty', 235
umbellifers, 295
upside-down fern, 269
Urticaceae, 271
U.S. National Arboretum hybrids, 159

V

variegated sweet flag, 215
Vegetable Garden, 29, 103, 106, 308, 312
Verbascum olympicum, 286
Verbascum/verbascums, 152, 280
Verbena bonariensis, 53, 70, 109, 117, 290, 291, 299
Vernonia novaboracensis, 216
viburnums, 186
Viburnum acerifolium, 192
Viburnum cassinoides, 186, 192
Viburnum dentatum, 192
  'Blue Muffin', 192
Viburnum dilatatum, 192
Viburnum macrocephalum f. *macrocephalum*, 191, 192
Viburnum nudum, 186, 192
Viburnum ×*pragense*, 235
Viburnum prunifolium, 192
Viburnum setigerum, 191, 192
Viburnum trilobum, 192
views, framing, 36, 118
Vigna caracalla, 114
vines and climbers, 221–222, 224–231, 229
Virginia bluebell, 277

Virginia creeper, 222, 224
Virginia spring beauty, 277
visitors. *See* guests
Vitis coignetiae, 229
Vitis davidii, 229
Voran, Laurel, 106

W

wallflowers, 53, 69, 70, 139
walnut trees, 16
watercress, 216
water features, 212
watering
    containers/pots, 28, 290
    in-ground systems, 290
    methods, 204, 290
    no-watering design, 290
    rainwater cisterns, 24, 202, 290
    suggestions for home gardeners, 24, 28
water lilies, 212
water plantain, 215
water plants, 212, 214–219
Waterwheel fence, 103
weathervane, 60
weeds
    ground covers for reducing, 24
    hand-weeding, 97, 208
    hoeing, 302
    invasive, 28, 92, 97, 113, 297, 299
    mosses as seedbeds for, 94
    mowing, 208, 209
    mulching, 204, 294
    planting to discourage, 97
Weigela, 186
Weigela florida
    'Alexandra', 184
    'Elvera', 184
    'Java Red', 184
    'Variegata', 179, 184
western red cedar, 114
wheat, 302
wheat grass, 262
white ash, 128

white clover, 202
white fir, 146, 149
white lace flower, 295
white oak, 101, 103, 122, 125
white pines, 16, 146
white wood aster, 274
wildflowers
    companions for, 243
    planting in mulch, 122
    trilliums as rock stars, 277
Wildflower Slope, 37, 264, 272
The Wild Garden (Robinson), 250
wildlife, 12, 212. *See also* birds
wild look, 116
willows
    chartreuse foliage, 136
    as olive-like, 79, 134, 302
    rooting, 135, 138
    silvery foliage, 79, 80, 302
    stems/branches, 53, 54, 135, 138, 139, 140
    yellow-leaved, 152
winter aconites, 238, 243
winter activities, 98–101, 103
winter and microclimates, 37
winterberry, 200
winter hazel, 186, 231, 235
winter rye, 63, 303, 306
winter rye grass, 262
Winter Shrub Border, 6, 144, 145, 249, 254, 280, 286
Winterthur Garden as inspiration, 166, 259
Wisteria floribunda, 222
    'Shiro Noda', 58, 222
Wisteria frutescens, 222
    'Nivea', 222
Wisteria macrostachya, 222
    'Clara Mack', 222
wisterias, 222
Wisteria sinensis, 222
    'Amethyst', 226
wood anemone, 31
woodland forget-me-nots, 250
woodland peonies, 275
woodland plants, 121

woodland sage, 72
Woods, Christopher, 18
woodworking, 101
woody plants, 92

X

Xanthocyparis nootkatensis
    'Green Arrow', 150, 152
Xerochrysum bracteatum, 117
xerophytic site, 37, 39

Y

yarrows, 290
yellow catalpas, 152
Yinger, Barry, 264
yoke-leaved amicia, 17
Yucca rostrata, 89, 90, 156, 200, 282
yuccas, 88
Yulan magnolias, 169, 170

Z

Zinnia spp. / zinnias, 156, 286, 292
    'Canary Bird', 292
    'Orange King', 292
    'Oriole', 292
zucchini, 308
Zuk, Judy, 169

The Gardeners at Chanticleer

BACK ROW, LEFT TO RIGHT   Scott Steinfeldt, Joe Henderson, Przemek Walczak, Jonathan Wright, Peter Brindle, Doug Croft, Ed Hincken, Bill Thomas.

FRONT ROW, LEFT TO RIGHT   Bryan Christ, Emma Seniuk, Anne Sims, Lisa Roper, Dan Benarcik, Erin McKeon, Fran DiMarco, Eric Hsu, Jesse Thomas.

....

DAN BENARCIK has been a horticulturist at Chanticleer since 1993. A native of Wilmington, Delaware, he holds a BS in plant science from the University of Delaware. He is responsible for the Entrance, the Teacup Garden, and the Tennis Court, and he introduced tropicals to Chanticleer. He oversees the woodshop, where he makes tables, seating, and railings.

PETER BRINDLE, grounds manager, was raised in Philadelphia, began working at Chanticleer in 1983, holds a BA in anthropology from Temple University, and is a graduate of the Longwood Professional Gardener Program. Peter oversees the horticultural and grounds staff, sings sweetly, and knew our founder, whom he calls "Mr. R."

BRYAN CHRIST is assistant facilities manager. He started as groundskeeper but switched to facilities in 2006. Bryan holds a BA in film from Temple University and an AAS in architectural engineering from Penn State University. He is our resident filmmaker, techie, web developer, rugby player, and musician.

DOUG CROFT, a horticulturist since 2000, is from Virginia and holds degrees in business and horticulture from Virginia Polytechnic Institute. He is responsible for the Parking Lot Garden, the Long Border, and young tree pruning. He is a ceramicist and an excellent cook.

FRAN DIMARCO came to Chanticleer as administrative assistant in 2005, following a career in the pharmaceutical industry. Fran's favorite aspect of the job is an afternoon stroll through the garden. She continues to learn more gardening terminology than she ever thought possible and is the only one of us fluent in shorthand.

JOE HENDERSON, horticulturist since 1997, grew up in Wilmington, Delaware, and holds a BS in plant science from the University of Delaware. He oversees the Pond Garden, lower Creek Garden, and Asian Woods. He is an artist in wood, metal, glass, and enamel, and a mushroom forager.

ED HINCKEN, a lifelong Philadelphia area resident, began as a painting contractor with Chanticleer in 1992. He became facilities manager in 1998, and uses his knowledge of energy conservation and sustainability in construction and maintenance. Outside of work, Ed's passion is rugby as spectator, player, and coach.

ERIC HSU, a native of Long Island, New York, became plant information coordinator in 2011. He holds a BS in plant science from Cornell University, an M.S. in taxonomy from the University of Reading (UK), and an M.S. in plant ecology from the University of Tasmania. He is our plant geek and a frequent contributor to *The Plantsman*.

ERIN MCKEON oversees guest services and our dealings with the public. A Pennsylvania native, she was a Chanticleer intern in 2009–2010. Upon completing her Master's in public garden leadership at Cornell University, she returned to be public programs manager in 2013. Occasionally, we find her smiling like the cat that caught the canary.

LISA ROPER, horticulturist, started at Chanticleer in 1990 following graduation from Longwood's Professional Gardener Program. A native of New Jersey, she has a BFA from Cooper Union in New York City. Lisa took over the Ruin and the Gravel Garden in 2013, after working on Asian Woods for a decade. She is our chief photographer, and raises chickens at home.

EMMA SENIUK was hired as a horticulturist in 2012. She is from Unionville, Pennsylvania, completed the Longwood Professional Gardener Program, and trained two years at Great Dixter in England. She is our newest addition to the full-time horticultural staff and is responsible for the Cut Flower and Vegetable Gardens, and the Orchard.

ANNE SIMS, assistant public programs manager, oversees the care and inventory of the Chanticleer House and archives and is our resident historian. Anne has a background in art history and previously worked for the Philadelphia Museum of Art, University of Pennsylvania Museum, and the Wharton Esherick Museum.

SCOTT STEINFELDT, assistant grounds manager, started at the garden in 2009. A native of Rochester, New York, he holds a BS in turf grass management from Penn State and a BS in business management from Canisius College. He wisely gave up golf course work for Chanticleer, where he oversees the grounds staff. He is our only Yankees fan.

R. WILLIAM (BILL) THOMAS started as executive director and head gardener in 2003 after twenty-six years in the education and horticulture departments at Longwood Gardens. He holds Bachelor and Master's degrees from the University of Wisconsin (his native state), is an avid plantsman, and writes about trees, shrubs, and vines. He lives with his corgi Jesse.

PRZEMYSLAW (PRZEMEK) WALCZAK, a native of Poland, has been a horticulturist since 1996. He holds an MS in economics and agriculture from Warsaw Agricultural University, and he gardens in our native plant area, Bell's Woodland and the upper Creek Garden. He sculpts in metal and wood, builds bridges, and is a punster. He is a certified arborist and oversees our tree care.

JONATHAN WRIGHT, horticulturist since 2004, hails from Unionville, Pennsylvania. He has a BS in Horticulture from Temple University and a diploma from the Longwood Professional Gardener Program. He is responsible for the Chanticleer Terraces, the Serpentine Garden, and Bulb Meadow. Jonathan enjoys cooking and loves plants.

ABOUT THE PHOTOGRAPHER

ROB CARDILLO has been photographing gardens, plants, and the people who tend them for more than twenty years. Formerly the director of photography at *Organic Gardening*, he now works for major publishers, horticultural suppliers, and landscape designers throughout the United States. Visit him at robcardillo.com.

CHANTICLEER

Wildflower
Slope

Ruin Gard

Gravel Garden

Pond
Garden

Rock
Ledge

Winter Shrub
Border

M

Asian Woods

Great Lawn

Bulb Meadow

Serpentine
Garden